# Joy Filled Souls:
# It Is Well With My Soul

## James E. McReynolds
### Minister of Joy to the World

Parson's Porch Books

*Joy Filled Souls: It Is Well With My Soul*
ISBN: Softcover 978-1-955581-74-5
Copyright © 2022 by James E. McReynolds

**Parson's Porch Books** is an imprint of Parson's Porch *&* Company (PP*&*C) in Cleveland, Tennessee. PP*&*C is an innovative organization which raises money by publishing books of noted authors, representing all genres. Its face and voice is **David Russell Tullock** (dtullock@parsonsporch.com).

Parson's Porch *&* Company *turns books into bread & milk* by sharing its profits with the poor.

www.parsonsporch.com

# Joy Filled Souls:
# It Is Well With My Soul

# Contents

# Dedication

To my loving wife Laurel, who has helped me
finish my unfinished soul.

The making of a book, as the making of the soul,
takes a lifetime.

# My Books Published by

## Parson's Porch Books

### 2011-2022

*The Spirituality of Joy: The Least Discussed Human Emotion, 2011*
*The Joy of Preaching: Encountering Jesus through the Word of God, 2013*
*Dancing with God: A Theology of Joy, 2016 The Silence of the Church: The Spiritual Struggle with Sexuality, 2017*
*The Spirit of Joy Church, 2019*
*Joy Comes in the Mourning: Love Is Forever, 2020*
*The Joy of Prayer: The Way to Intimacy with God, 2020*
*The Joy of the Kingdom: Envisioning the Great Commission, 2020*
*Walking with God in the Garden Journey in Jouissance, 2021*
*Joy in the Seasons of Life: Walking Each Other Home to God, 2021*
*Living the Dream: Amazing Adventure in Marriage, 2021*
*Joy Beyond the Walls of This World: Healing the Souls of Men . . . and Women, 2021*
*The Gospel of Joy: Global Impact of the Ministry of Joy to the World, 2022*
*Joy Filled Souls: It Is Well with My Soul, 2022*

# Foreword by Dr. John Killinger

I have to say it. I'm blown away by this book. I've ready many of my friend-and-former- student Jim's books, but this one, as special as all have been, is really special. Nobody but Jim would have thought of writing a book about the soul. Not today. The Greeks and Hebrews talked a lot about soul in ancient times, but our society has grown away from such weighty concepts.

We talk instead about egos and personalities and centers of being, but not souls. To us, souls have become amorphous—mere references to our existence and not to anything more.

Jim has taken us back to a more religious and embracing concept of who we are, of what constitutes our being, and dared to write about his favorite subject, joy, as it relates to this hallowed and ancient concept. That's what blows me away. It is a daring and enormous undertaking. By reminding us of this old and revered idea of who we are—who each of us is – it challenges us to review everything we know and feel about ourselves.

I am writing this foreword at a heavy time in history. The Covid pandemic has been wreaking havoc for more than two years. The number of deaths in the United States alone tops the one million mark. Most of us have lost at least one friend or loved one to the dreaded virus. The whole world is convulsed by its presence. The war in Ukraine has been transpiring for months. Our TV screens and constantly filled with scenes of the horror it has wrought on the poor citizens of that valiant country. And yesterday came to news of the awful massacre at a school in Uvalde, Texas, where nineteen children and two teachers lost their lives. The air around us is palpably thick with grief and suffering.

On top of all this, our little Maltipoo named Toby has been requiring veterinary service for doggy diabetes and infection on his leg that has been slow to heal because of the diabetic condition. My wife and I are emphatic: Some days we suffer more because of Toby's condition than he does.

As I lay in bed thinking about all this in light of Jim's book about joy and the soul, I asked myself, "How is my soul adapting to all the pain and hurt in the world right now? Can I find any joy in what I know and feel?"

The answer was, "Yes, there is a somber kind of joy in my soul, my wider being, in spite of all the horror we're experiencing in the world. It is not a jump-up-and-clap-your-hands kind of joy. Far from it. This joy offers a kind of comfort that rises from the depths of my being, a remembrance of good times and lightheartedness before all the suffering began, and a confidence that some of these things will return when the suffering has waned and once more faded into the background of my consciousness. That will happen. It always does.

I shall not forget the atrociousness of this particular time. It will remain embedded in my memory for as long as I live. The bad will be absorbed into the good again. I shall once more turn my thoughts to love and fellowship and the wellbeing I generally know in my life. My soul absorbs life and history and yet manages to remain intact and positive despite what is happening at this juncture in time.

I consoled myself and went to sleep under the weight transpiring around us. It was not an easy or comfortable sleep as I usually enjoy. And this morning, reflecting on it, I understand that Jim is right to remind us of the importance of the soul and the joy that informs it even in the worst times of our lives.

I stopped writing to go down to the kitchen and fix myself a cup of coffee, which I usually enjoy. While I enjoyed my coffee, I noticed an unusual amount of anxiety in my heart. When it did not get better, I realized I was having a panic attack.

I had never had one, as far as I know, but I recognized this one from things I have read about them and from listening to reports of parishioners through the years.

I took some deep breaths and reviewed the things that were weighing on me—the pandemic, the war in Ukraine, the reports of the mass killings. The panic did not subside.

I thought about Jim's book and something I read in it. He wrote, "We dread the dark valleys, but they are steps to joy." They are the steps to joy because they lead us to pray, to be with God in our inner beings. And being with God, opening ourselves to the divine power of healing, is the secret to a wonderful, fulfilling life.

Remembering Jim's words, I stopped to have a time of prayer. Soon I was feeling better. The panic subsided. I felt at peace with God and my own life. Jim's words were healing. There is still joy in our souls when the way seems dark and foreboding.

I hope other readers will find similar comfort in this special book. It is an important book for our time.

Dr. John Killinger

# Chapter One

# Souls Sharing In The Life Of God

Human beings are the top-of-the-line spiritual product designed by God. This book's cover shows a human body and the soul. The journey of the soul through our human life is an opportunity given to us to experience being alive in several dimensions. This book's theme is the often-quoted words, "We are not human beings having a spiritual experience. We are spiritual beings having a human experience."

We exist because of divine design. We do not know about our purposeful path consciously.

The goal of the unfinished soul is to feel existence. The soul path is not to overcome life's anxiety and struggle, but to know life fully, to exist in context. (Thomas Moore, *Care of the Soul: A Guide for Cultivating Depth and Sacredness in Everyday Life*, p. 260)

God reveals our calling. Different souls are attracted to differing things such as cooking, music, sports, writing, or parenting with a sense of soul gratification. This state of elation puts humans in touch with the highest energy for soul lifting. Joy.

When we find that inner call and follow that joy, a miraculous phenomenon happens. Unique gifts open. Once we know our gifts, they are to be shared with others to continue the ebb and flow of love through each of us. The Divine Force nurtures us, binds us collectively, creates new life, heals, and takes our soul back home.

Each soul is like an enchanting divine flower in a divine bouquet. When each flower blossoms in its full glory, the result is an eternal masterpiece.

We long for companionship with God. Our souls need to share in the life of God. Our life journey is not walked alone. God walks with us. Talks with us. God comes in intimacy. Every soul has moments when we share this intimacy. We can't explain, and we cannot explain it away. William Blake wrote: "He who binds to himself a joy does the winged life destroy; but he who kisses the joy as it flies lives in eternity's sunrise."

Traveling the world keeps me wondering and questioning. I have encountered many differing types of people. Travels stimulate soul-searching and transformation. The children of God, believers and unbelievers are complex.

Each is looking for how to exist in the earth. We learn from all the other billions living as we wait and listen. Only spiritually mature persons enter the kingdom of God as a little child.

When Dalai Lama and Desmond Tutu were asked to write a book on lasting happiness, they choose *The Book of Joy*. Tutu came to visit His Holiness for the Dalai Lama's 80th birthday.

Douglas Abrams asked pointed questions and Adams guided them to share their wisdom.

Each morning, we find joy in a sunrise. No two are ever the same. Each viewer sees a different color. Pink-orange sky reminds us of the breath of God.

These moments come in mysterious intuition as God touches our lives like a soft hand of the morning sun. Insight.

Understanding. Moment of grace. Awareness. Faint sounds. Respect. Wonder. Souls see beyond the surface of life.

My Laurel and I have enjoyed hearing Paula D'Arcy speak and we have bought most of her books. Paula was like a sister and friend to us as she reached out to us to share her insightful thoughts. She asks some deep questions: "What if the soul we declare to be invisible, caged somewhere inside of us, is actually the thing that defines and contains us?

"What if we do not make our soul more or less acceptable by our virtues or good deeds?

"What if the soul has never been away from the heart of God?

"What if the soul, the true child of God, labors so that our human nature can find its way back to being a true image of God on the earth?

"What if the Spirit has the power to create and labor even under the limited conditions imposed by matter?

"What if the Spirit continues this work, whether or not the human heart and mind can consider or accept it?

"What if faith I the forerunner of true seeing is actually an act of seeing?

"What if we had the desire or courage to find God where it counts the most, in life?

"What if we knew that within our very cells is a God- given energy, a source of light that possesses the secret of God's beautiful and complex design?

"What if we understood that from this hidden place (his secret nature) comes everything that is?

"What if our hearts desired to know?" (Paula D'Arcy, *A New Set of Eyes*, pp. 123-124)

The Hebrew word for soul can be found 755 times in the Hebrew Bible. The inclination of Hebrew is to use the same word for a variety of functions that are labeled with distinct words in the English language.

The Hebrew is not "the immortal soul," but it is simply the life principle or a living being. Read Genesis 1:20-24. "Nephesh" applies to the creation of humankind where dust is vitalized by the breath of God. His can mean the corpse of an individual even if dead. Soul is a desire for God. Read Psalm 42:1-2.

In Hebrew language a mortal is a living soul rather than having a soul. Instead of splitting a person into two or three parts, Hebrew thought sees a unified being.

"Psyche" is the Greek New Testament word translated as soul. The letters of Paul he often uses "soma or pneuma."

"Psyche" indicates the person is used in Acts 2:41. Read Matthew 10:28. Soul is an immortal part of the body.

There are also shades of meaning of soul and spirit. The inner flesh, that which breathes, her or his own flesh, belly. The soul and belly are consumed by grief in Psalm 31:10. As life-breath, the soul departs when we die. Read Genesis 35:18, Jeremiah 15:2, Psalm 16:10, Isaiah 38:17.

Soul can stand for an individual, a person, or a personal life. Anima and animus are Latin Vulgate terms for life inherent in the body. Animus means mind, the center of mental activities.

As part of your own biblical studies, phases such as hungry soul (Psalm 107:9,) weary soul (Jeremiah 31:25,) a loathing soul (Leviticus 26:11,) a thirsty soul (Psalm 42:1-2,) and a loving soul (Song of Solomon 1:7.) Dealing with questions about soul are part of most Hebrew studies in seminaries.

At both ends of life, we ponder eternal questions. In our youth and childhoods, we focus on the future.

We wrestle with life decisions. In our later years, we face a challenge to slow down and anticipate sharing life with God.

Dallas Willard wrote: "Our soul is like a stream of water, which gives strength, direction, and harmony to every other area of our life. When the stream is as it should be, we are constantly refreshed and exuberant in all we do, because our soul itself is then profusely rooted in the vastness of God and the Kingdom." Quoted by John Ortberg, *Soul Keeping*, p. 15.

Every moment of life is filled with the presence of God that bestows and loves. To live by faith means to see this pure love. Every moment of your life is a moment of meeting with God who is loving you.

God links grace to each moment. God draws good even out of evil. The consequence of our sin gives fruit in the form of an opportunity to be converted.

Grace is the expression of love. Every moment is filled with love, even during our most grievous sin. We are always emersed in the love of God.

Everything the soul experiences is tied to the love of God. God wants everything to work for our good.

## Happiness and Joy

Happiness evolves from one's personality. Joy is of the soul. Joy filled souls are experiencing a deeper level. When we become in tune with the soul, we always experience joy. Even when everything appears to go wrong, we have "the joy of the Lord as our strength."

Happiness involves all our emotions. Being happy is ephemeral as a result of some happening that pleases us from shifting moments. Joy springs from the eternal. Joy is an inner state rather than a momentary response to something that is external. Joy filled souls aspire to live each moment of each day in the true authentic joy. Don't let the joy pass you by.

Take a walk. Breathe deeply. Gaze at the trees and flowers. Listen to the songs that birds sing. Look up to the clouds in the sky. Eat a nourishing food. Hug your child or grandchild. Give thanks for the soul is made for endurance.

Innocent joy is found in a four-leaf clover. Joy is like an undiscovered waterfall. Joy is finding a unique rock picked up in place where we traveled. Sing, talk, and croon to the flowers and plants and waters. Put your feet in a creek or stream. Nature never loses its radiance. It helps us live the mystery. Joy is a fruit of patience.

Identifying what lights our fire calls for paying attention to specific things that enliven us. We feel lighthearted. We are present to the moment.

Curiosity is aroused. We lose track of time. Find what lights your fire, your zest for life. Finding ways to be open to God's love fills us with grace.

The journey of the soul is infinite. The path each soul takes will be unique. The diversity of soul paths is limitless. God celebrates our individualism which each step taken on your soul journey. Failures, setbacks, and mistakes are never an end. Each experience is valued for the narrative of the journey. There is a balance. We experience the good and the bad. We discover and learn. Our unfinished soul is supported by love. Free will is paramount, and we are given that control, because it is our own journey. Safe travels.

## Intuition

Intuition is mysterious, powerful, and subtle. We are born with intuition. Intuition creates expression of the awareness of the soul, the consciousness of soul of a higher truth that humans are immortal and wise. Incarnation into a human body and an earthly journey give the soul diverse experiences. These generate the gradual accumulation of wisdom.

Evolution of an unfinished soul interacts with other human souls. Challenges are faced. Lessons learned. Qualities develop. Wisdom is the goal of the soul.

The Holy Spirit perceives life in a large perspective, with a global and universal vision of becoming aware of our origins, original nature, and our relationship to the source of all life. This inner guidance in the unfinished soul makes possible the knowledge of ourselves, our purpose, our highest creative potential. Intuition leads us to ourselves, to God, to home, to the ancient wisdom of the soul.

My ancestors, people with my DNA, my spirit guides, my appointed angels, mentors, and my intuition empower us to live wholesome lives. These guides include our spouses, and our children, grandchildren and great grandchildren enable us to transform confusion into clarity, heartaches into healing, and fearlessness into genuine enthusiasm. Soul guidance is universal to everyone. It comes from human intuition. Willingness to keep our minds open and acceptance of surprises comes with intuition, our original sense of inner knowing. (Judee Gee, *Intuition: Awakening Your Inner Guide*, pp. 1- 40)

"I love intuition. I love its mystery, its depth, and its truth. Guiding others to the revelation of their own intuition is a delicate, powerful, and blessed work, a process in which I participate with respect and gratitude." (Ibid., p. XIX)

During my own vision quests I seek to know who I am. Why am I existing now? What is happening and what will happen? Where am I going? These questions are part of my search triggering the initiatory journey within myself. Soul seeking does not involve the rational mind.

Souls must dig deeper. The gift of intuition involves memory, knowing, and belonging. Intuition is evidence of divinity incarnate. Intuition is the tool for finding our place and purpose and for reconciling ourselves with a living, loving, guiding presence we perceive with inner senses.

Intuition includes obstacles such as overthinking, approval seeking, should, and trauma. During my time of writing this book, I am involved with a clinical psychologist and a coach in a "Learn to Live Program," sponsored by the Pension Fund of the Christian Church (Disciples of Christ) in the United States and Canada. Intuition is when one makes decisions devoid of analytical reasoning, replaced by emotional information and insight based on experience. Humans use both analytical reasoning and intuitive thinking. Intuition is pattern-matching.

Insights we get from intuition enter the conscious awareness of what we know or think we know. The soul holds deep seated experience that gives way to the best decision. Intuition is learned expertise in disguise. I played tennis in my youth. G.B. Pierce, my coach at Tennessee High School, and Coach Dickinson at Carson-Newman, taught me to go with my instinct on the court instead of thinking through each stroke.

Intuitivism may cause a feeling of being lost or confused. Intuitives describe it as feeling being pulled between who they should be and who they are meant to be. They think they have lost themselves in roles to the point that they don't know who they are. The soul ultimately tips the balance toward change, towards a more authentic stance in the universe.

We need to affirm the love of God for us. As we march forward in our journey to joy, we feel God working through us, accomplishing the will of God. Love answers a deep need inside every soul for nearness to God.

The unfinished soul focuses on externals, lives to consume, pleases itself, and is purposeless.

The unfinished soul sees no worth and feels valueless. Morality is subjective and arbitrary. Unfinished souls are never content or satisfied. Unfinished souls are whimsical. They imagine purpose from relationships that promise intimacy.

The love of God energizes human existence. When we "turn our eyes toward Jesus," our self- centeredness becomes other-centeredness, temporal to long-term results, self-esteem to servanthood, existence to direction, immediacy to ultimacy, and appearance to realities.

A finishing soul is becoming alive. Freely. Enjoyably. Meaningfully. Spontaneously.

Purposefully. Joyfully. Lovingly. Eternally. Finishing a soul includes intense commitment and exhilaration, deep craving for God, extreme love for God, and joyful enthusiasm. Read Luke 6:46-.

Love is sharing in the life of God. That is soul passion. A soul will die for what she really loves. God is our passion, our ultimate love.

Joy filled souls find it impossible to separate loving God from loving others. Our unfinished souls become nearer to God when this love expands to others.

With deep love for God, we perceive the world through new eyes. The world becomes not just the place our needs are met. This earth is the spot where we can give to others who have needs as well. Love is limitless as it belongs to the Creator. This love crosses social and ethnic boundaries, international boundaries, and cultural division.

The pastor of the First Baptist Church in Boston told me, "I believe in the fatherhood of God, the brotherhood of all humankind, and the neighborhood of Boston." God's love has no city limits, denominational limits, neighborhood boundaries, or national borders.

Love lasts. Every person living now will die. Brick, mortar, and steel in buildings, churches, schools, and homes will be gone. Churches are being torn down for lack of use. Hotels and office buildings are built on the sites. In the tiny town of Union, Nebraska, there remains the First Baptist Church of Union. Records show that it was the first Baptist church built in the Nebraska Territory before Nebraska was a state. People gathered in homes for worship. In 1880, the church building was erected. The lovely church stands today with a beautiful sanctuary, padded pews, a classic organ, and many features any congregation would envy. The church belongs to the American Baptist Churches in the United States. They have preaching service once a month and only one family attends. The town once had a high school. They keep the old school building with wire fences around it. It now looks like it was bombed by Russians. The school won the state championship in basketball in 1909.

When we pray or read the Bible, we are reminded of love that makes eternal life possible. We are finite, limited, and we are like one grain of sand on a beach. Contemplate the many billions of grains there are. We could not gather all the grains in a million lifetimes. He riches, joys, and love of God are beyond understanding. We spend a lifetime exploring just a tiny portion of creation.

Maya Angelou said, "If you're going to live, leave a legacy. Make a mark on the world that cannot be erased." Placing God at the center is the key. The desire for God is inside our soul. It can never be erased. Separation from God causes life to lose meaning.

The movie, The Trip to Bountiful, an elderly woman was seeking a home long gone. It was a home of her childhood, youth, and early married life. No place on earth could satisfy her longing.

Souls are looking for a deeper sense of the presence of God in life on earth. We hunger for the good news that God is present working for our good in all things. We probably are not hungry for heaven, but we long for heaven on earth. Heaven is our home, but heaven begins here and now. Unfinished souls find bridging the gap between heaven and earth, bringing heaven down to earth. Souls get a taste of heaven as they walk on earth. Read II Corinthians 3:17-18. The Holy Spirit's work of transformation begins here and now. We long for the peace of God and the love of God. "When we all get to heaven, what a day of rejoicing that will be."

Imagine how frustrated God is with us. God views all that is possible and yet we squander our souls away. God wants heaven for us more than we want it for ourselves.

Each person is unique. Some aspects of God you alone appreciate. Eternal joy will be to communicate our personal surprising joys to each other.

# Chapter Two

# Souls Surviving By Faith

Joy isn't a feeling. It is faith. Souls sharing in God's life become new persons. Read II Corinthians 5:7.

My brother-in-law, Roger Bornemeier, lives in blindness. I understand this verse both literally and spiritually. Roger navigates the world without sight.

Surviving by faith means to keep moving even if we do not know where we are going. When we read Exodus 1, God is leading the Israelites out of Egypt. Instead of traveling the easier and direct route, God leads them through the wilderness.

God knew what was ahead. It was a better journey for the people. Read Exodus 13:20-22. The people did not know where they were going. They kept moving and they looked to God for guidance. God did not choose to heal my 88-year-old Roger. God chose to deliver him from his hardships and grief that his disability brought.

Without full sight or a pillar of fire for guidance, Roger turned to his faith. Read II Corinthians 4:18. Roger learned to use the small dimness of his eyes to work miracles. He even rode his lawn mower slowly into town to do what he had to do.

Walking by faith and not by sight means that we live today according to the promises of God, even though we do not see them, and not according to the temporary thigs that our eyes often focus on.

We trust God even when we cannot see God working on our behalf. In our faithing, we doubt that God is listening. Facing difficulties and praying relentlessly, we may think God has abandoned us.

God's hand is evident as we read the book of Esther. God's name is not mentioned I this book. Esther was made queen miraculously. God gave her courage.

God softened the heart of Mordecai at the right time. God gave relief from their sorrow as we read the book to its ending.

We find a new comprehension of reality, a new perception of God, and our intuition sees temporal reality in a brighter light. Souls survive as we accept that God has created everything. Faith is fundamental to all supernatural life. Faith gives us the possibility of sharing in the life of God. Faith is sharing in God's thinking. Faith is synchronizing our thoughts with the thoughts of God. Read I Peter 1:8.

This mysterious fresh thinking leads to contemplation and introduces us to future knowledge of everlasting life. We penetrate the life of God and Jesus. And God begins divine life with us. Faith brings a complete change from our former ways of seeing, thinking, feeling, and experiencing. Our mentality changes. We place God first. We focus on God. We interpret the world in the light of God.

Communion of faith realizes its fullness in love. This oneness illuminates our desires, appraisals, judgments, and aspirations. Souls survive by encountering God.

Faith allows us to discover the trace of God in Creation. God waits for us to experiencing everything in faith. Everything is meant to serve towards our sanctification. Everything is grace. Only when we stand before God will everything be clear to us.

Faith in the New Testament is the human response to the revelation of God in Jesus the Christ. Faith is sharing in the life of God. Faith is sharing God's life within us. This allows us to see ourselves and the reality surrounding us as if we were seeing it through the eyes of God. "Faithing" permits us to rely on Christ for our salvation. God's love and mercy bring forth the joy of heaven.

Sharing in the life of God through faith causes us to become a finished soul. The soul can then notice the Presence, the creator of everything. "Faithing" allows us to keep in touch with God. It is sharing God's thinking. It means to synchronize our thought with God's thoughts. We are introduced to a finished soul both now and in our future knowledge of God in eternal life. Through faith, God begins the divine life within us.

Faith accomplishes in us a complete change from our former way of experiencing, thinking, feeling, and seeing. The Light of faith illuminates all judgments, desires, and expectations. A communion of faith is then established which is realized only in love. The created world surrounding us is a voice speaking to us. If our faith is weak, the voice will distract us, pull us away from God's love. This voice in the world becomes a place where we encounter Love.

Every moment of our lives is filled with God who loves. "Faithing" brings us to accept the will of God. God links grace to every moment. Grace is an expression of Love. When we see God in everything, our prayer will become a prayer of faith.

We are always immersed in God's love. Faith is a different way of looking at the world. Faith allows us to know God in the phenomena of nature. Christ gives us talents for us to take proper advantage of. Everything is a gift.

In our children and grandchildren, we celebrate their progress. We hug them, kiss them, clap for them, congratulate and reward them. They deeply known that they are loved.

An environment of encouragement creates improvement as unfathomable. Bringing children with us to church makes possible an intimate conversation with God about what we are learning, our talents and abilities, our dreams, or failures, our potential, and love for all people including our families and those who come close to us.

Souls must be finished, perhaps in heaven, as we become ourselves. Our life journey paves the way to be in inner dialogue that encourages our growth every day. The unfinished soul views failure as part of success. We can pause and take time to identify what we learned from the experience.

Differing circumstances awaken the sense in different people. The personal circumstances shine a light upon what we need to do next. During some of these moments, we are vulnerable to this phenomenon. Some may be seized by guilt and inadequacy that they immerse themselves in work or travel to share our concepts of gospel. These seekers return to their own lives with the vital questions still lingering. God has created us to be where we are in the present moment for specific reasons. Regret is the sand trap of the soul. Where we are is where we are. Where we are going is up to us.

Letting go of some dreams is bliss when many dreams will not be realized. We accept who we are and where we have been, which saves us from regretting the life that was ours.

Stand still. Renew courage. Be quiet. Stay where you are. God has something wonderful to occur inside the unfinished soul. Search for ways that are real, tap our intuition, and awaken our imagination.

Being ourselves never leads to the destruction of our soul. From the moment of our birth, we are searching to understand and struggle to reveal who we are. As we leave our childhood, we may shift away from the God-given identity. We begin to move toward drawing our identity from their surroundings of place and people.

Most children and even adults want to please our moms and dads. We attempt to impress them. We want them to be proud of us. My parents have died, but I still feel that I must impress them.

Unhappiness is the fruit of doing and saying things that contradict who we are and why we are here.

Unhappiness is not something that happens to us.

Unhappiness is something we do to ourselves. Unhappiness has an unlimited number of ways and reasons to be unhappy.

Happiness is different. Happiness is sustained beyond the experience that produces it. Happiness, which includes joys, has the still voice of God guiding us. The voice reminds us that something wonderful is about to happen.

Unfinish souls wish their lives away. They wait for some future experience that they have fantasized will erase problems and cause

25

us to be happy. These souls are missing out on life, moment by moment.

Do the next right thing. And act without hesitation. Consult with God for all your decisions.

## Handling tense situations.

Everything is meant to contribute to our sanctification. Everything is grace. Only when our unfinished souls stand before God will everything be made clear.

Handling tense situations sometimes ends in failure. Failure is a priceless treasure. It finishes our souls.

In the gospel of joy, the master returned from his travels. He demanded an account from his servants. God will one day ask us how we used our times of failures.

Difficult graces are the most valuable experiences of the soul. Faithing is sharing God's vision of reality.

Faith sees every day of life as Jesus sees it. We will find unceasing opportunities for conversion and sanctification. We recognize our crosses as opportunities for transformation.

Imagine what it would be like to judge ourselves with the thoroughness of God. Immense joy would come as we discover that we are known, accepted, and forgiven.

Learning to love others without possession, control, manipulation, conditions is what it is to receive this gift and to be surprised by joy.

Joy is related to our deepest desires. The unfinished soul chooses joy again and again. Giving up a present good for the promise of a greater joy requires faith and risk. To know that one is a sinner, and simultaneously to know that one is standing in the grace and love of God is the essence of joy.

**Faithing makes us grateful for everything**.

This thankfulness will be visible on our faces as joy. Everything can be changed into good. Read Romans 8:28. God is never sad as life gives us failures, problems, unfulfilled plans, everyday difficulties, and spiritual hurdles. because God expects all things to bear fruit. We will be joy filled and grateful for all things.

I appreciate how God has used my speaking and writing. Sometimes I prefer writing to speaking. Both gifts feed on each other. I love my life. I would not trade it for anyone else's life. I do what I love. I know satisfaction and joy in my calling.

I enjoy speaking to high school and college students. What a miracle to have written and preached more than 120 high school baccalaureates. My message is for them to focus not on that age-old question, "What do you want to do when you reach maturity?" I ask them, "What is God inviting me to become?" To minister for their joy, the Spirit invokes me to stress doing to becoming. God has bold dreams for every student. God has plans that are bigger than they can comprehend. God's dream is for us to use what we are passionate about. Whenever I speak to students, an hour seems like ten minutes. When I sit down in my home study to write, the next thing I realize is that I have been writing for four or five hours, but to me it's like I sat own just twenty minutes ago.

I enjoy ministering with student. My longest time in any one place of work was 20 years as the campus minister at Southeast Community College in Lincoln. In a Bible study session, I asked students to consider two of their classes. One you love, one you hate. The class you love passes in a flash. The class you hate drags on forever. The class that is loved represents living in your passion. The hated class represents quiet desperation.

Life is about love. I have loved spending so much tie with young people in high schools and colleges. I know how important it is to find their passion before they make life choices and commitments. Passionate life is best worked out during the years of youth when they are single, young, and uncommitted.

Some people cannot do what they love full-time. Find what you love and do it.

Faith in the subjective is not only sharing in the life of God, but faithing is an existential obedience to Christ Jesus. Faith implies that every soul makes a choice. Souls steer their way and will toward Christ as the final goal and number one priority.

Obeying God is the beginning of love. It is a personal and community communion with God. This requires a free heart, a turning way from sin. Read Matthew 6:24. We will be tempted to compromise and combine that which can never be combined.

When we take stock of what we are thinking about most often in our prayers, we will see what our greatest treasure is. As a creature made by God, we can choose to attach ourselves to the will of God.

Everything that enslaves us or keeps from trusting in God diminishes faith. (Dean Ornish, *Love and Survival: Eight Pathways to Intimacy and Health,* pp. 25-44)

Faithful prayer can only develop in freedom. It is essential to have a free heart. Difficult moments and life's storms are graces. Christ is the giver of our total freedom. Spiritual life is realized under continuous tension between the will of God and personal wills. Our lives revolve on our wills. And we revolve around what is convenient to us. Our plans and interests we want; does not correspond what God wants. The events in our lives often demonstrate how God foiled human plans so that human beings could unite with the will of God. The Holy Spirit is capable of descend upon a person with graces that will ruin all plans.

Faith is relying on Christ and trusting ourselves to God. Searching for security can be illustrated with scenes from college life. A student taking an exam bases her security on memory of what she has learned or on her intellectual abilities. She could count on luck. All human systems of security cannot be perfect. They are based on our calculations and plans. When human systems fail, we will face disappointment. Christ gives our only security. Faith relies on nothing apart from God.

God watches with joy the miracle of human faith. God has the right to request that we give everything, everything in the sense of total trust. Jesus appeared in the world with absolutely nothing. We are like the lilies of the field and the birds in the air, which God loves and cares for.

The plea in the Lord's Prayer, "Give us this day our daily bread" is a call to deepen our faith. This day.

Not tomorrow. Not for a week. A month. Any future time.

An unfinished soul who reaches union with God and is sanctified is a person who has accepted Christ to the end as the only love. To love means not only to give but to accept the love of another person. God's unconditional love wants to protect us from everything that becomes a threat to our freedom and faith.

One reason I write books is to explain my life to myself. When I do, I find I am explaining other people's lives to them. The earliest memory in the videos of my mind was during World War

This first memory occurred as I lay on a couch in our small apartment located above a grocery store and across from Woodlawn Baptist Church in Bristol.

Life was tense for everybody. My dad was serving in the army in the South Pacific. My aunt was living with my mother. I remember my aunt and my mother being angry about something. My first emotions felt were of fear and anger.

Joy was never part of my unfinished soul. That is why I have studied and written so much on joy. I wonder how we all survived those early years of my existence.

# Chapter Three

# Souls Completing Sanctification

Sanctification is a heavy word. Most ordinary people have little idea of what it means. One way to define it is unfinished souls being finished.

We will all keep having questions about why life is as it is. Sanctification is being a work in progress. A sacred delight fills our souls as we live believing that God is faithful. Read Psalm 62:5-8.

As we believe God will complete the good word the Creator began in us, we can trust God in the next thing that is planned for us.

God meets us where we are, just as we are. As we confess our sins, God restores and forgives.

As we release our imperfections, God comforts us.

Making of a soul, like love, requires a miracle, and the appropriation of miracles requires faith. Intimacy takes time. Marriage takes time. Vows promised at the wedding speak to this need of dramatic community "for better, for worse, for richer, for poorer, in sickness and in health, till death us do part."

Love requires the kind of commitment that assumes a future where things night get better or worse. Nevertheless, the love goes on. Making of a soul as well as the making of a lover requires receiving into life the mystical rather than the problem solver.

Soul making pays attention to the invisible things we cannot control. It is not a problem to be solve, but a mystery to be lived. Finishing an unfinished soul requires moving away from desiring to control waiting on the mystery at the heart and center.

To finish a soul means to know what I do and to survive to struggle and achieve. To make a soul is to live in time with its opportunities and limitations. Our lives are stories that unfold in time. God created the world out of the sheer joy of living.

The inability of unfinished souls to reach out and touch each other brings suffering from a deformed sense of self. Love requires a miracle because the world conspires to encourage or to seduce us to define ourselves as other people's expense. Love is not diminished from sharing it.

As we rest and regroup in God's presence, we weep over what wrecked us. We pour out our hearts to God about how we wish things were different. Consider experiencing God differently and trusting more. Finishing a soul is the removing of masks and setting us free as we enjoy the life of God.

Realize the power of rejoicing.

Rejoicing in the Lord is easier when we have good news. Read Philippians 3:1.

Safeguarding our faith . . . sanctification . . . is serious work. If we only allow our faith to thrive when things are to our liking. Faith causes us to rejoice in Christ's redemption.

Faith is the reality of what we hope for. It is evidence we cannot see.

Read Hebrews 11:6. Faith takes us beyond our comfort zones. Faith develops in us a Christ-like character. We focus on the reality of God.

Keeping our focus on God is essential to protect faith's ability to function. If we lose that focus, faith becomes in short supply. Rejoicing is our source to realize that whatever happens to us is subject to the power of God. There may or may not be much joy in my circumstances, but the joy of the Lord is our strength.

God holds us together in a kingdom in which each individual provides the context for the flourishing of each of the others. Each contributes to the beauty of the whole community of faith.

Joy comes to us in our times of sorrow. As we receive the truth of God, God's joy fills us with delight. Joy overflows when we walk in faith and obey. God is the giver of joy. All things become possible. As we regroup in challenging times, your joy will take us through any and everything. (Gregory Jones, *Embodying Forgiveness: A Theological Analysis*, pp. 109-114).

When we feel that our soul suffers from lack of joy, we are seeking short-lived pleasures and substitutes for everlasting joy.

Joy is a choice, a decision to do and say things that ultimately free us from sin, heal old wounds and trauma to open our hearts to love. Joy chooses to practice compassion with others, God, and our selves. Joy filled souls choose to spend time with people who bring on smiles and laughs, who help us feel safe and supported.

Joy is choosing to make our needs for love, belonging, and acceptance important enough to finish our souls during this lifetime and always.

Joy honors our creativity when and where we can. Joy chooses the positive side in midst of pain and suffering. The soul's existence makes art, dances, skips, runs, jumps, shouts, and soars. Joy listens to the Holy Spirit's direction to live to the full expression of human potential.

Joy comes down to a lifetime of choices that lead to love and to realize what's best for you.

Retirement is a mixed bag.

The changes are exciting, yet unsettling. For years, we have been energized with new opportunities to use our gifts. Retirement can bring on self-doubt. Colleagues promise to keep in touch, but rarely do. We look back and don't know how much our career was worth. Couples spend more time together. They must begin to know each other again. Who are we now without our roles? We all desire to be joy filled souls.

Retirement can bring loneliness and losses. We now see that all our dreams were not possible. Time is running out and our lives appear to be incomplete. Keep swimming in the direction of joy as it flows. Relax in the love of God and flow with the eternal stream.

That's why I spent time with Dr. Robert Kunz for counsel so I would not damage the people I love. I also found healing in the program of the Pension Fund of the Christian Church.

Nicole Jeffreys served as my coach to facilitate changes in my thinking, my exercise, and the essentials of how to live. She asked me questions about what was working and what was not working in my lessons.

The love of God brings us to the joy-filled instincts that guide the world. It is never too late to recapture the passionate longings we were born to experience. Never underestimate the potential. Never lose hope. Never stop trying.

Unexpected miracles are standing in front of us.

Why don't we see them? We ignore the possibilities of our souls with closed eyes. We must uncover what we have forsaken to find what we are searching for. We do not have to make efforts or travel far away to discover something more beautiful than we can imagine.

# Chapter Four

# Souls Facing The Dark Desert

The soul is the deepest expression of the person. Dark nights are of the mind, or the will, or the spirit. A monk named John coined the phrase in the sixteenth century in Spain. He ended up in prison. From his cell, he wrote *The Dark Night of the Soul*. He said the dark desert time feels like the silence of God. The Bible turns to ashes. Practices that have fed the soul, nourish it no more. Souls are required to learn spiritual meekness.

Luke Skywalker in "Star Wars" was awakened with the words, "May the Force be with you." He was instructed not to let his anger to open him up to the dark side.

Souls are transformed in the dark desert. They are changed. For better or worse. Dark depression is burying the soul into the ground. Souls wait in darkness, alone, solitary, silent, waiting for a coming spring.

When we drive our automobile, we begin when it's still dark. The windshield looks clean and transparent. But when we arrive to where we work, the sun is shining. Al the smudges and deflects are visible. Finishing the soul is like that.

The closer we move toward the Light, the more our intense our souls are exposed. The graceful Light of God will clean and healed.

We dread the dark valleys. They are the steps to joy. Struggling through that valley teaches us humility.

We are reminded that we are vulnerable, small, frail, mortal, complicated. Dark nights create an atmosphere for prayer time. During deep valley experiences, we are forced to regroup, reflect, to rest. We whisper our secrets to God as we do to a close friend. There

is nothing in the dark night that we cannot face. Nothing will be given to us that we
cannot bear as souls were made for the valleys. Keep this life stage in clear focus. It is not a bad thing to be where we are.

Relax. People develop their own character. Life is the only environment. We are able to change our automatic reactions to the environment, the atmosphere, the context, or to other people, or to God. Souls that know passion for God are eternal optimists who live in chronic joy. Relaxation is needed to restore our souls. Rest is not a sign of laziness or weakness, but a sign of wisdom. As my office sign says, 'Don't let joy pass you by.'"

Resting does not restrict joy. Rest sets us up for more joy. Rest leads to joy for we are still, still enough to hear what we miss. In thee nourishing quiet times, souls will appreciate the gifts that we have taken for granted. Imagine living in the present and not fretting about the past or future.

Today will shimmer with an afterglow of a revived soul. We gain differing perspective on our struggles. God in gracious providence is at work, we live in joyful surrender and with wonder. Don't postpone your joy. Choosing joy is not naively thinking everything will be easy. Joy is courageously believing that there is still hope even when life gets difficult.

**Free tickets to a life play.**

Joy filled souls are given tickets to a play. With the sunrise, the curtain rises, and we experience another scene. These scenes do not last forever. As an 80- year-old, I have seen 29,200 daily parts of the scenes of my lifetime. These scenes do not go on forever. It is as long a play as I want to review in heaven. The enthusiastic play watcher would grow weary. When we leave the theater where we have seen the life- play, the stage is as dark and blank as before the play started.

Life goes on after death. We have trillions of cells and equally trillions of universes. Life is too well- arranged to be meaningless.

In my own experience with depression, I know that only in the dark soil into which the grain falls, and the soil out of which grows the fruit.

Entering the wilderness, souls face spiritual hunger and thirst. Spiritual bread is needed in the wilderness for life is uncertain. Securities are lacking. The soul wandering possesses nothing. Relying on God is the only answer. God desires to become everything for the soul traveling in the desert.

Depression can be a gift. I treasure it, and I live my life not only out of a sense of appreciation but out of in indebtedness. Another fruit found when I suffered exhaustion and was brought to a safe haven was the knowledge of how little control I had over my own life. I was given a depth of intuition to hold on until the storm passes.

Intuition will show us that wisdom cannot come through the borrowed knowledge of others, but through our own deep understanding.

The dark night of the soul is an unsettling, confusing, and difficult phase of inner transformation. We travel in dark woods with limited visibility. It is a spiritual process intended for

souls to develop capacities to awaken the integration of ways to live. We must do something different.

Anatole France said of eternal joy, "The average person who does know what to do with his life wants another one which shall last forever."

Our unfinished soul must live between effort and surrender. He must not resist the direction of the wind. The dark night is our plan for living, our vision quest. Our vision quest serves our souls. It is the path to awakening the deepest parts of our souls.

Journaling is how my creative juices flow. Write at the top of today's page, "What needs to happen for me to feel more vital in my life?" Perhaps exercise. Thought inspection. Active problem solving.

Assertiveness and boundaries. Dwelling and sleep habits. Adventure. Nourish the connections in our relationships. I am always asking, "How can I best contribute my gifts to the world?"

Souls at elite places know darkness.

John Cook, who has a 90 per cent winning percentage as a NCAA Division One volleyball coach, shares his struggles with burnout and mental health. Coach Cook's soul entered a dark night.

Cook realized that he did not feel as one is supposed to feel at the top with multiple national championships. He felt empty. One morning he said, "There is no more joy in this."

He could not sleep. He was exhausted and filled with anxiety. His moods swung like he was riding a roller coaster. His doctors couldn't help. He sought specialists. He even traveled to Rochester, Minnesota to be examined at the Mayo Clinic. They gave the volleyball genius test after test. These doctors finally said the bottom line was his stress.

His therapy plan included cognitive behavioral therapy. Coach wants his story to reach his teams, to us volleyball fans that admire him, and to the world. Cook asked Tom Osborne, three times national champion football coach, how he handled the stress of his job."

"John, I didn't. At age 49, I suffered dark nights and a heart attack." Professing his faith, Osborne is a United Methodist Christian. He suggested Cook pray and meditate. Cook paid closer attention to nutrition, sleep, breathing, and recovery.

Cook paid attention to little and big things. The stress of Nebraska volleyball will never go away. The Huskers lost in the national championship match to Wisconsin.
To any other coach, this would have been highest success.

Nebraska fans expect to win the national title every year. The dark night of his soul forced John to make a daily plan to manage the stress. He improved his diet. He even gave up coffee. He goes on automatic with his meditation and times for prayer.

Mental health issues also challenge the young athletic women, ages 18 to 22, who obsess over winning, losing, roster spots, tests, classes, dating, and a million little things to juggle. Endless pressure, a do-or-die attitude to be the elite are an unforgiving syndrome. Like some churches, universities fire their leader almost every year.

That is why we all need to meditate. Your mind and body must calm down. If not, your career ends sooner than you had planned." His soul was filled with joy. He does not fret over wins and losses, expectations, or pleasing other people. This shift in thinking is why he enjoys coaching more than ever. Coaches, pastors, physicians, or others must make changes to survive.

## Failure and the Desert Experience

Beginning in kindergarten, we are socialized to compete. We begin with grades, awards, being best. It was beating others out. We cannot just stop. Every win or loss forces us up or down. Success was the motivation word.

In the breakthrough book, 1984, George Orwell introduced us to "doublethink" and doublespeak. People can say one thing and mean another. Lying by a government is called "a program of misinformation."

Deception becomes "fake news" or managed news. The decision to doublethink is true of many pastors. "Nothing sells like a winner" rich, cunning church leaders say. How do we sell the gospel that insists the first will be last? The rich will be sent empty away. The power will be pulled down. The meek will inherit the earth. Modern church growth programs find it hard to resist.

In the early church discipleship meant failure. Accommodation was appealing. The church has ministered to the unintentional failures. The chief image for failure became the desert or the wilderness. John the Baptist went into the wilderness to preach and to do ministry.

Failure is a harsh word. It is a difficult to accept reality. Failure is avoided and is a source of fear. We attempt to soften the harshness.

We suggest failure in normal. Failure is not really failure. Failure is transformed into a catalyst for success.

Failure is not just a matter of losing the big games. It is losing the coaching job. We try to pump up our optimism. We say, "I may be down, but I am not out." Failure is a dark experience that causes us to believe we are inadequate. There is a looming shadow over our soul. Failure colors the landscape of our lives.

Failure is a spiritual crisis. It is not our ultimate enemy. Biblical stories like the woman at the well or the man by the Sheep Gate pool, and the younger son in the prodigal son saga, that shows how much better it is to face the failure, feel its pain, learn tis kernel of truth, and faithfully trust the God continues to give new birth.

Carlyle Marney, a Southern Baptist minister with a strong voice, shared a story in his sermon during the student chapel at Carson-Newman. It comes to mind when I am in a dark place.

He told of a young girl who lived at the edge of a dense forest. She enjoyed walking in the woods to explore and go on imaginary adventures. One day near dark, she got lost. She began to worry. In the gathering night, her parents searched for her.

This child tried one possible way out after another, none looked familiar. None appeared to lead her back home. Her arms were scratched. A limb caught in her hair. She continued to stumble and fall. Her makeup streaked over her face. Black oozed over her cheeks. Coming to a clearing, she lay by a ragged rock and dozed off to sleep.

Her parents keep searching and calling her name. Her mom gave up and so did some neighbors. Her dad kept searching all through the dark night. As dawn brought light, her father spotted his daughter quietly asleep. As he called her name, she awaked.

She rubbed her eyes. "Daddy," she cried out, "I found you."

Our Father might meet us in a dream. God sees our fears and our tears. The forest is never so deep. Our Dad comes to us where we are. God speaks our personal language. Christ calls us into and out of the wilderness.

Our Father (or Mother, if it is more to your understanding) creates from our unfinished souls on an empty canvas. The Word desires incarnation into our lives. The Word comes on tablets of stone and the words from the Bible.

God's words are found in unexpected places and the unluckiest people. Souls must become accustomed to the unaccustomed words and ways of the Father.

Writing articles and books has been an exhilarating joy, and every time I finish a book, I rearrange deck chairs to accommodate my sprawling passion.

I have also discovered that publishing books was not a romantic nor easy cruse as the travel brochures make it out to be. Read Habakkuk 3:17-19. My role as the Minister of Joy to the World has kept me in the know that cold winter is followed by spring.

During the years I was writing for the Sunday School Board, I would make journeys for the purpose of disseminating the 22 programs of ministry. Because one of the programs I was assigned was National Student Ministry, I enjoyed going to the campus sites.

I was drawn to the Baptist Student Union at the University of Southern California in Los Angeles and the creative campus minister Milt Hughes. One of the participants was a young man named O.J. Simpson. He was the star running back on the Trojan football team. I interviewed O.J. and he expressed a love for God. We prayed together. I assured him that I would continue my intercessory prayers on his behalf. I wrote several news articles and a feature for Baptist Press which was published in secular newspapers and denominational state papers.

Years later I was shocked to learn of O. J's dark night of the soul. Ego rather than love dominated his unfinished soul. The nation followed his career in professional football with Buffalo in the

National Football League. What a tragedy that he replaced his popularity, good looks, money, and fame for the love of God.

# Chapter Five

# Souls Sensing The Voice Of God

Soul awakening to the voice of God arrives as we realize that material things are not satisfying. Something basic is missing. We must acquire listening skills that allow us to hear. God's unique voice reveals our essence. We are sensitized to aliveness, to genuine grief and sadness that are part of being alive as are joy and jubilance.

Life is wonderful but brief. Souls meditate on death as they do not take precious life for granted. Life slips through our hands like water. We must live boldly and faithfully by listening to that gentle voice within.

Souls know a deep desire to make a difference and to be of service to God and humankind. We realize our roles are important, but we do not wish to be defined by them. We sense that we must express something from an inner urge deep inside. Our souls long for meaningful relationships that are authentic where we can share ourselves with like-minded souls. We feel discomfort as we are being drawn into the unknown without any idea how it will happen.
Souls awaken to understand the language of the soul. That's the nature and integration of the voice of God. The soul is the truth of who we are. It is time to make friends with our unfinished souls.

Our souls are hungry and need to be nourished to flourish and thrive. We are feeling an inner urge to shed outdated ideas about what it means to be a faithful person. We are being transformed into a way of being that aligns with our souls. We realize that we are a spiritual being having a human experience. A wise person is someone who has learned to listen to the voice of God.

God knows that we need to belong to a loving community. As I have traveled the world, I am convinced that the local church gives us a role in creating a vibrant loving community.

Everybody wants to belong to a dynamic church. Most are not. Members of congregations ignite continuous support and learning and working to make the local church a perfect place for perfect people trying to walk with God. Our Father will empty our souls of useless attachments, superficial desires, and ego- centered inclinations, so together we can fully love God and the people who cross my path.

Each moment is another opportunity to love.

God's voice is meant to be heard. Christians have forgotten their Jewish roots. The common way we approach the Bible is in silence. This approach was unknow in the Jewish tradition.

Speak the scriptures. Notice how we now comprehend the meanings. Reading the Word of God aloud makes it easier to remember and memorize.

The biblical message comes alive when read aloud. The words jump off the pages. Our inner ears and our souls take them in. The imagination is inspired. The words of the text are incarnated as we read. Our senses are ignited with understanding. The Word is a megaphone that is heard in the depth of the soul. The reading opens the door for taking part in scripture and being part of it.

What an inspiration to hear the living Word in Jesus' own words. Reading and listening to the Word allows us to learn and capture what is in the mind and thoughts of God.

Silent reading is better than no reading at all. Sometimes we are not in a situation where we can read loud. We still hear the Voice of God.

Read John 6:63. Also, read John 10:3-4, Revelation 3:20, Job 23:11-12, Luke 24:44-45. Ponder them in your heart. Meditate on John 5:37-40, along with Isaiah 55:10-11.

Every moment of each day, God and your inner soul are sending messages designed to empower us to live in wholeness and joy. With the voice of God, we are sensing the transformation from confusion to clarity and fearlessness into enthusiasm as "we see through a glass darkly."

Sensing the voice of God is fundamental to remembering our magic to create helpful synchronicity in the atmosphere of your life.

Every time we override God's voice, the soul gets louder. God never stops trying to get through to us. God's gentle guidance could come from a persistent thought. A guiding dream. A book. A blog. Physical symptoms. Gut instincts. Bumper stickers. Synchronicities.

Reconnecting with the Still Small Voice is medicine for the soul.

When I look back on my youth and I see reminders of who I was, and hints of who I was to become. I see our backyard snow forts and baseball mitts. I had scores of cigar boxes filled with Topps baseball cards. If I had kept them through the years, I would be a millionaire today. I see soda and coke bottles rattling around in a red wagon. My brother Ed and I used to pick up hundreds of bottles on the beaches of South Holston Lake near Bristol. We sold them for two cents a bottle. Bike riding was a joy as playing cards (and baseball cards) were clothes-pinned to the spokes. My dad made me some stilts that I walked on in those days. My father also built a go cart with a seat long enough for six people. We pushed it off to ride down Jonesboro Road in my Bristol neighborhood.

I recall stacks of comic books bought in my childhood days. Looney Tunes, marvel comics, and comics about Roy Rogers, Gene Autrey, Randolph Scott, Bill Boyd, Hoot Gibson, Allen Rocky Lane and his horse Blackjack, Rex Allen, Charles Scarette, the Durango Kid, Cisco and Poncho, the Lone Ranger, and Hoot Gibson.

Some of my childhood friends still have their collections.

Reflecting on those years of joy, I hear something calling my name. We grow such glad souls as we follow the Christ. I have unearthed the passions of my heart that were there buried in my youth. Let me go back again.

Unfinished souls think about future. The name of God could be Joy. "It is well with my soul." As I think about my journey with God, I am pleasantly surprised by God's love. Whatever happens, we shall all be well. At the funeral of my dear friend and colleague, Dr. Robert Kunz, our regional minister in Nebraska quoted

Romans 8:35-38. These words took our breath away. We shall be well with our soul no matter what happens. God's love will move us into the future with renewed assurance. This is the joyful surprise of the infinite love of God. Read Revelation 3:20.

The kingdom of God is wherever God's Spirit is present and welcomed. When believers gather, they know God is with them. They gather for prayer, prophecy, teaching, laying on of hands, reading of letters, and the gathering lasted until midnight. Acts 20:7.

Some hear the voice of God as they read or hear the Word of God. We hear the voice of God with conscious minds. Some hear the Voice with subconscious minds. They listen with inner ears and see with the eyes of God.

Living in the present moment, God guides them intuitively. To hear God, we must be plugged into the power source. Faithful souls are already connected through Jesus the Christ. Fine tuning is required to hear the Voice. Read I Corinthians 2:14. Peter preached the essence of the Spirit will appear by quoting the prophet Joel in Acts 2:16-18.

It is God's desire to speak to the hearts of individual believers and the whole community as they gather. God speaks quietly to the heart, or God speaks loud enough through human lips. Hearers are filled with the fruit of the Spirit.

# Chapter Six

# Souls Connecting By Prayer

Prayer and faith are not separate realities. Prayer is always connected with the reality of faith.

Prayer is meeting with God in faith. Prayer is the giving of oneself in complete devotion to Christ. Faith is acknowledging our helplessness. (See my book on *The Joy of Prayer: The Way to Intimacy with God*, 2020.)

Effective prayer is kingdom-oriented prayer. Kingdom people look to God alone as their patron, and to the kingdom alone to sustain them. As God answers our requests, we experience here and now a foretaste of the everlasting kingdom. (Alan Street, Heaven on Earth: Experiencing the Kingdom of God Here and Now, 268-269)

Christ Is Our Best Example.

Read Mark 1:35. Notice the detail: "Before dawn." Jesus deprived himself of sleep. Jesus prayed in solitude. To know if your contacts with people has yielded fruit, we must know before how to be secluded from others. Souls need to know that nothing is more important than connecting in intimacy with God. One tragedy of our activism is that activities smother us.

Nothing is as important as God in our lives. God does not need human intervention. But God wants to involve us in the redeeming work of saving the world. Read John 3:16.

Prayer is being present to God.

In my older years, I pray in reminiscence. I look back on my memory tapes and enjoy seeing how God has used the good and bad to finish my soul. I empty myself from bitterness to allow the loving God to get access to my soul. My prayer has become rooted in the understanding that God unconditionally loves us. We inhabit our life more fully. Is it better to live well or to live for a long time?

Prayer must be our priority. Contact with God determines the value of our work. The issue of prayer is the major issue in our vocation. By praying, we are paying homage to Christ on our behalf, as we worship him in the name of the whole world. If we do not pray, nobody will need us. The world does not need empty souls. All authentic action is born of prayer and intimate contemplation.

Prayer is the crucial issue for every soul. Prayers are signs and indications of our closeness or distance from God. We want to feel closer to God. Souls wonder where God is in times of tragedy. We strain to hear the voice of

God when we search for direction. Souls feel distant if it has been a long length of time since we had an uplifting prayer experience. Read Psalm 63:2.

Our prayer hunger is like snow falling on the deserted field of our lives and our hopes become frozen or lost. When we are down, we are tempted to stay down. We become unable to find our way back. We feel frozen in mind, body, and soul. Read Philippians 3:12-14.

Robert Redford, Jennifer Lopez, and Morgan Freeman made us aware of missing the mark in the movie, "An Unfinished Life."

I wrote in the introduction to my book, *The Joy of Prayer: The Way to Intimacy with God*, on page 15: "Are you enjoying intimacy with God? The Westminster Confession of Faith stated, "the chef purpose is to glorify God and Enjoy God forever. Prayer is not a remedy. Praying becomes a living relationship with the living

God. Sharing the whole of our soul is tough work. All of us struggle with prayer. We want God to be closer, to be an intimate companion, who is always present in our lives. We want to be silent with God and knowing God with all our senses. I wondered if God was longing for me. I want to share with you how my own understanding, experience, and practice of prayer have expanded. I have enjoyed bringing all I am becoming in relationship with God. I pray with my body and soul and my journey never stops. I pray this book will stir the fires of your own desire for God, encourage you in your own searching." Ibid., p. 15.

We feel so good when we feel the presence of God while we are praying. Prayer can then be something appealing. We are convinced we are only praying to God. We will discover the fuller truth about prayer, like a musician who lost her hearing. We become deaf in contacting God.

Our prayers become fully free from self-interest.

When we begin to experience a state of dryness in prayer we do not yield to the temptation of resignation. We must continue to learn to pray. It is a task as we try to pray in our words and language.

Faithing has an influence on what we pray for. Read Mathew 6:33. That word "first" is important. God wants us to continually simplify our prayer. Prayer of quiet thought is an expression of faith. The One who loves us is always close to us. Jesus loves us. As the Christ, the Father loves all those in our community that we care about.

We learn to pray best when we think we cannot pray. The secret prayer in our dark nights is being hungry for God. God hunger comes from a deeper place than our feelings or words. We are then helpless and humble. When we are unable to pray, the Holy Spirit comes into our souls and prays for us. Read Romans 8:26.

During that time God sees our soul stripped of its own strength, the joy of the Lord becomes our strength. In my carefree youth, my prayer life meant talking to God if I could find the time.

Reading the Bible, I discovered that Jesus was at home with solitude and his interior world. Jesus spent entire nights in prayer. Read Luke 6:12. He prayed in Gethsemane before he was crucified. He spent forty days in prayer in the wilderness. His soul was so united with the Father, so God's presence went with him wherever he traveled. Being with God in a daddy-child relationship forms the core of the living soul.

My friend and mentor John Killinger wrote that Jesus built a reservoir of strength as he communicated with God. (John Killinger, *Bread for the Wilderness, Wine for the Journey*, p. 65)

Killinger taught a class on Prayer at Vanderbilt Divinity School. Students found an inner calmness as they yielded to the will of God and became one with the love of God.

We do not have to do anything. We trust God is there. Let go and let God. Permit God to be there. Let what happens happen. Distractions.

Wandering minds. Let yourself be human and weak. Stop demanding. Cease complaining about whatever problems living in our world may bring.

Celebrate the reality of what is there.

Our unfinished souls in our own vision quests shift from the thoughts about complaining, whining, and demanding to a place of receiving and celebrating.

We begin to look at life differently. We delight in all that we perceive. Our souls slowly transform into beings of gratitude. Read I Thessalonians 5:18. We are in for a surprise, a joy.

When my daughter was with me in the car, as her loving father, I would buy a little gift for her and place in the so-called glove door. She always knew that there was a surprise for her hidden inside. There was a gift she could not imagine. We both discovered that God is a Father of infinite surprises. The greatest needs our souls need is the love of God.

Prayer is the breath of the soul. Prayer unites our souls with God in our thinking. As we turn toward God along with all our life activities, we are given a disposition for unceasing prayer.

The channel of our souls is cut deeper and deeper. One of the misconceptions about deeper intimacy with God is that we don't need other people. Awakening our souls, we no longer see people as an inconvenience. We begin to look deeper into faces. We begin to be more attentive to others. I became more thrilled with their joy.

When we respond to other people as if they are Christ, then they become my sister and brother.

We move into close association with other souls in an unusual understanding. When we are struggling, we need a friend to hold the lamp for us until we can pick it up again.

God in our own lives can be visualized by others. Amazing miracles happen when we love others as God loves us. The more we are one with God, the more we are united with one another. With our deeper identification with other people, God sends us all words of joy.

Hope. Clarification. Comfort. Meaning. These words often come from others.

Within community, we find love. We find we belong in the world. Earth is not filled with strangers. Community is a coming together that puts us in touch with the soul. God is not quantitatively more present with two or three people than with just one. More than 20 occasions, I have communicated though preaching to only one other person.

Often in my Clergy Support group gatherings, only three attends. Somehow the Spirit of God is there to give us a surprising word from God that adds to our joy.

A small touch can spark community and a sense of God. Experiencing God in a spontaneous community requires that we become willing to allow people, even strangers, the get access into our souls, and together we know moments of intimacy and love.

With O.J. Simpson and other troubled souls, I took them into myself, my joy, where I encounter God. In prayer then, I bring them into the presence of God. By my act of will and imagination and intuition, I am with them.

Recalling my times of prayer for my patients housed in the Lincoln Regional Center, disturbed people descended from my mind and into my being. I did not have to list their needs. God's Spirit prayed within them and for them. I gave my own energy and "the joy of the Lord" on their behalf. Our compassionate souls are expandable. God does not limit to those who dwell with us, as God's love knows no boundaries. We release them to God. Only the joy and memory remain. The fulfilling joy of being loved by God makes it impossible to separate love of God from our love for others.

When my daughter Linda was born, I went to look at her in the Nashville Memorial Hospital nursery.

Something opened deep within me. In 1970, fathers were not present at their child's birth. I had never experienced the intimacy and love of a father. That day I was keenly aware of the Father within me, working through my soul to become my daughter's daddy. I was awakened with joy and a renewal of the intimacy of the love of God.

God wants to lead us to places we cannot journey to without the power of the Holy Spirit. Prayer is a doorway to heaven on earth and in the Next Place.

The joy of intimacy means God living in your soul.

Your dreams become in juxtaposition with the dreams of God. We can communicate in intimate communion that is familiar and comfortable. As our souls enjoy God, we can pray: "I believe that the desire to please you does in fact please you. And I hope that I never do anything apart from that desire, And I know if I do this, you will lead me by the right road, though I may know nothing about it.

Therefore, I will trust you always though I may seem lost and in the shadow of death. I will not fear, for you are ever with me, and you will never leave me to face my perils alone."

Enjoying God is the soul's greatest delight. Jesus told us, "The kingdom is within you." The joy of God is infinite and unspeakable. God's loving blessings are unfathomable.

Julian of Norwich noted, "Prayer fastens the soul to God." Prayer is the deep joy of intimate companionship that arrives step by step until we know the oneness of love. Grace moments sweep us away with the joy of communion with love. Love is divinity dancing inside us. Every moment in our earthly journeys is a sign of the kingdom coming to us. Intimate prayer places our soul's attention on every blessing we receive as the years go by, and we find that we are in love with God.

Love is not a one-way encounter. God loves me too. Baptizing new converts, I hear them say that they have fallen in love with God.

Love is the condition of our existence. To be a creature of God is to be in love. Praying makes us aware of love. The joy of praying enables us to become aware of the times of joy. God is always with us encouraging, waiting, and calling.

In the Next Place, there will be no tears, no disease, no war. The soul will possess incredible freedom, a sense of lightness. With Jesus, we will think with the mind of God. Our desire will be fully known.

Love brings energy into the world that we can receive and give to people who are starving for love.

When we turn our minds to God, God invites us into a loving relationship that is unique and unending. Love is forever. Prayer restores humans into the image of God. By sin that image was obliterated. A refurbished transformation brings truth, beauty, and wisdom. These wash into our unfinished soul.
Without our prayer connections, human beings lose their identity, our likeness to God. We become blind to the gospel of love and forgiveness.

God invites us into a deep life of prayer so that God can fill us with a joy that nobody can take from us. We need the things that cannot be taken away. That joy will not be fleeting or short-lived.
Always take your first opportunity each day to spend time in prayer. Prayer leads to spiritual health. Spiritual health has rewards s we tend to be full of love. Focused. Invigorated. Generous. Patient. God

desires to bless us with spiritual health. Few things delight me more than sharing with you what God has freely given to me.

My dear readers, every day I pray for you. I imagine you sitting alone somewhere considering the thoughts on the pages of this book and the pages of other books I have written. I pray that you will have the joy of finishing your unfinished soul.

The Gospel According to Thomas did not make it into the canon. Most of it appears to be an inspired book. In it, Jesus is saying, "The one who is near me is near the Fire." That fire is the love of God that purifies us. This Fire consumes us as if is undisguisable from the Fire.

We read about God refining us in the fire as silver purging our sins. The image of fire at the day of Pentecost when the followers of Jesus were praying.

In Acts 2:30, the imagery of tongues of fire to describe the coming of the Holy Spirit.

Suddenly a sound like a rushing wind filled on those present. Tongues were a "fire of joy." The fire represents the presence of eternal God.

Fire is a symbol of sanctification of the unfinished soul. Fire is contagious and difficult to contain. When the fire of the Spirit consumes our souls, it is impossible to keep the gospel of joy within ourselves and our communities. God needs people who are filled with anointing holy fire. God commands us to spread the Word of God like wildfire in the world that is starved for love and joy.

Flames flickering bring thoughts of passion and desire. Fires leap. Fires dance. Fires spread with abandon. "Fiery passion" and "light my fire" means someone has inspired passion with somebody's soul.

When a fire rages, the old growth in the forest burns away to allow a new forest to emerge from beneath like a rebirth and a resurrection.

In our final years when our strength diminishes, we can live zestfully and continue to pray and do what we can do to finish well.

Warming God's children with passionate fire is one way to describe our life journeys. In my book, The Joy of the Kingdom, I composed a poem for what a minister of joy does. "Like fire, I gain energy from the moments of joy as I fan the fire. Like fire, I generate heat and light. Like fire, I expand to all directions. Like fire, I dance with God. Like fire, my thoughts ascend to heaven. Like fire, I burn with hunger for the joy of a finished soul. Like fire, I am deeply involved in my life experiences. Like fire, I am filled with creative passion. Like fire, I consume people with intensity. Like fire, I warm people by using my passionate joy.

This fire inside me continues to move, stretching upward as if awakened from a refreshing nap. My fire keeps renewing its energy. "It only takes a spark to get a fire going, and soon those all around can warm up in its glowing. That's how it is with God's love, once you've experienced it. You spread God's love to everyone, you want to pass it on."

# Chapter Seven

# Souls Growing By The Word Of God

A close interdependency exits between faith and the Word of God. Reading scripture requires faith, conversion, and cooperation. The Word gives life flowing from faith. Faith is response to the Word of God. See my book, *The Joy of Preaching: Encountering Jesus through the Word of God*, published by Parson's Porch Books, 2013.

The Word of God can be addressed in two ways, like an object we examine to find a solution to a problem that interests us. The other way is personally, as a subject. The text becomes a mystery. When we read the Bible with the intention to broaden religious knowledge, that means that we regard the Word as an object.

This is not sufficient.

We gain knowledge of God. The Bible is an inspired text and a source of revelation. Our relation to the revealed text is a personal one. The Bible is not a thing. It is a Somebody who is alive and present. When hearing and in reading the Bible, we encounter a living Christ through the gift of faith.

Biblical evidence about Jesus is compelling. The Bible was written a long time ago. Many conclude that it is filled with contradictions and historical inaccuracies.

Truth is told in many forms and genres of literature. The Bible contains a variety of them. To interpret the Bible properly, we must understand the literary form of a passage. Jesus makes use of parables. The Good Samaritan and the prodigal son are not named and could be cited to teach truths about mercy, charity, or the love of God. Jesus used hyperbole, a form of literary exaggeration. Read Matthew 5:30. The remedy for sin is not literal, physical amputation. Jesus' use of that figure of speech to express a sense of urgency in renouncing sin. Some parts of the Word are to be taken literally. Biblical writers used non-technical language.

"Divine revelation" is the term used. Read I Thessalonians 2:13. Martin Luther wrote, "The Bible is alive, it speaks to me, it has feet, it runs after me; it has hands, it lays hold of me." The Holy Spirit to inspired 40 writers in 1,500 years to write the Word of God. "Inspire" means to breathe into. Read II Timothy 3:16. God's breath gives life. The books of the Bible at we rad were in the canon. Canonizing is the process that church leaders used to choose what scripture was to be used to make up the Bible that we use today.

In the first centuries after Christ, councils met in prayer to determine which books would be included. The Old Testament had been canonized. So today we read 66 books as the Word of God.

When I send a completed book to a publisher, I simply email it. For centuries, we used printing presses fore that miracle, books had to copied by hand.

God used Hebrew and Greek.

God did not lead the authors to use other languages as the major languages that were used to explain concepts or to tell God's stories. Hebrew was the language of the Old Testament. God used Hebrew words for its true and pictorial, and personal language. After my studies with Dr. Kenneth Wolfe and Dr. Pierce Matheny at Midwestern Baptist Theological Seminary in Kansas City, Missouri, I fully realized that Hebrew perfectly describes how God is involved with human beings.

Greek is the primary language of the New Testament. Greek was the language spoken by most of the then known world. Greek was the ideal language for transmitting the Word from God.

As we read through the Holy Scripture, we sense that the soul was designed to reach for God. The Hebrew Bible covers this thought. Read Psalms 25:1, 33:20, 63:8, 143:6. Our souls live in God. They will never rest until they rest in God.

## The presence of God in the Word

When taking the Bible in our hands, we enter a realm of that Presence. It is mystery for you.

Contact with the revealed text has special meaning for our souls.

We will find Christ in the Bible. It is a way to contact God. This leads us to inner conversion. If we enter a person-to-person relationship with Christ, who is present throughout the inspired text, the Word will permeate us. We begin to listen intently to the Word. We will understand the desires and thoughts of Jesus and start to know him better. Our decisions and choices will be in line with his teachings.

When we read the scriptures, we might not think of a time to talk to God. Praying the scriptures is being with God as we read them. We gain insight and guidance initiating our intuition. We need a receptive attitude when we read the Bible. As we interpretate, exegete, and examine the Word, we must listen and receive what God is saying. Ask God to be with us as we read and open our souls to receive his message. Wait for God for what God wants us to see. God is coming to us here and now.

Of course, the Bible describes old history. These biblical accounts describe events that are occurring in every life now. God is speaking to us right now. Jesus' parables are in my live now. he acts of Christ are moving in my life now.

There are now more than 7000 languages spoken in the world. The Word has been translated in less than 2400. God has carefully planned for the preservation of scripture throughout many ages. These carefully translations bring the Word from God. The Old Testament was the first known work that was translated into other languages. In the second century after Christ, it was translated into Greek.

This translation was known as the Septuagint. Jews and Christians enjoyed this version. In the third century, Latin replaced Greek as the common language. The church had headquarters in Rome. Jerome completed a translation of the entire Bible in the year 405, which he called the Vulgate. It was a thousand years later, that the Word was translated into the English language.

The Latin Bible was the only translation used in the church. Hundreds gave their lives to translate so we could have the English Bible. John Wycliffe, a professor at Oxford University in 1384, was the first to translate the Word from the Latin. Martin Luther translated the Bible into German n 1522. William Tyndale devoted his life to translating the Bible from original manuscripts into the language of common people.

He finished it in 1530. He king of England had thousands of copies burned. Finally, Tyndale himself was burned at the stake in 1536. Miles Coverdale and John Knox produced the Geneva Bible in 1560. It was regarded as the only reliable translation. It was the Geneva Bible that the Pilgrims brought on the Mayflower in 1620.

King James the First did not like the Geneva Bible. He then appointed 47 people to create an authorized version of the Bible in 1611. He called it the King James version.

Having a Bible and reading the Bible are not the same. Most everyone reading this book have a Bible in their home. God chose written language as the primary method of communicating. Studying the Bible is not a substitute for reading it. To study the Bible, most means "to be eager and diligent." Read II Timothy 2:15.

A little baby is nourished by its mother's milk. Babies prefer it to any other milk. Unfinished souls drink in the spiritual nourishment provided by God's Word. Read I Peter 2:2. God gives each person free will to interpret what the Bible means. Read James 1:22 and Galatians 1:6-7.

Reading and interpreting the Bible is a spiritual venture between you and God.

Spending time and attention in the Bible each day will be a source of changes in your soul.

You will not continue to be the same. You will experience joy as you change. The Word gives us a glimpse of the love God has in store for you. In most seminaries and divinity schools' students are introduced to a scholarly discipline called textual criticism. The reliability of ancient texts is the focus. The New Testament uses no original manuscripts. No manuscripts of any writing until the modern era have survived. Ancient documents were written on papyrus that decayed over time. Scribes made copies. In Latin classes, we read Gallic Wars by Julius Caesar. It was written a century before the New Testament. We have no original copies. Only ten ancient texts exist, dating from the year 900 A.D.

We can use our imagination to place ourselves into the story. The soul responds to images as our inner emotional and spiritual language.

Morton Kelsey led a seminar on preaching told participants to use imagination to journey into biblical scenes. We will gain a sense of contact with the Presence to penetrate hidden truths.

Kelsey wrote, "When prayer and meditation concentrate on our concepts, they do not touch the most profound part of our being. Conceptual thought does not have the same power as the ability to think in images." Morton Kelsey, *Transcend*, pp. 82-83)

Reading the Bible is a fundamental factor in our growth in faith and in sharing in the life of God. If we attempt in faith to share in the thoughts and desires of Jesus, then they will eventually become your thoughts and desires. Our intense contact with Christ, who is present in the Bible, will cause us to identify with Jesus even more.

Allow this truth to overwhelm you. Learn to listen intently. The purpose of our lives will be achieved as Christ is increased within us and we will reach the fullness of joy.

No documents of the ancient world are as well attested as the 5,366 ancient manuscripts and fragments, all datable to within fifty to one hundred years from the originals. (Josh McDowell, *The New Evidence That Demands a Verdict*, pp. 30-38)

When Luke writes of the travels of Paul, he mentions various people and events. These facts can be known through non-biblical sources.

The New Testament has been tested more than any other text. It has withstood the scrutiny of friends and foes.

God desires intimate conversations. The wonder of this motivates us to open the Bible in expectation of hearing the Voice, not as duty, but as delight. We race through a passage and the distractions of daily life hijack our thinking and steal intimacy with God.

Reading the Word and the Word reading us stills our racing minds and welcomes the Holy Spirit.

# Chapter Eight

# Souls Fulfilled By Love

Love is the subject of the songs we hear on the radio. Love burns in the pages of novels. Most movies and television shows are about love.

People are searching for love. They surf channels. They scan stations. They open a book. They call movies and books "love stories."

God quietly gathers in love the frayed edges of our lives. Love. That's soul passion in a word. What we love, we follow. God is our ultimate. weaves the threads of difficulty, challenge, failure, success, blessings together. Romantic love will not be enough with a couple for a lifetime. Physical beauty fades with age.

Attraction often diminishes as romance becomes routine.

Deepest love between two persons resides in the level of the soul. The mysterious part of us is accessed through kindness, goodness, and love's expressions. My wife Laurel and I believe that we are soulmates. We intuitively communicate in the level of our souls. We often transcend the barriers of words as we embrace in divine grace. This intimacy imitates, nourishes, and deepens and our human needs for love are completed. His happens when we are in an awake condition.

Life is a soul's first gift. Love is the second. Finishing and understanding our soul-making is third. We must treat our souls with gentleness and tenderness. We wonder and we ponder about the existence of life. We protect each other.

Because we are made in the image of God, we were created to love the way God loves. At the end of our earthly lives, our souls desire such love. God wants us to experience that eternal love now. Unfinished souls begin on earth to live by the standards of heaven. Love becomes a natural habit.

Love drives us to noble deeds Love allows the spirit to push against impossible odds. Love creates a soul passion. Even in the dark nights of the soul, love prevails. Love overcomes the option of quitting. No matter what the situation is, love prevails.

Loving people may die of old age, but they are forever young. We accumulate friends of every age, some older, some younger, especially the friendship of children. The capacity for friendship is endless. When we extend or receive the gift of friendship, we are treating others as our equals. As we gaze at another, we are looking into a mirror to see a reflection of ourselves. Giving and receiving love makes us more alive.

Keep a journal or a notebook. List your acts of love. Include your kind words, your appreciation for a task well done, lifting another's spirit, giving a warm smile, giving compliments, being nice. Your list will grow longer every day. Nourish all your relationships, especially with God. Relationships require work. We need to connect with positive people who will be our support as we ride the peaks and valleys.

When we love and help others so that they become better for themselves, it is also better for us. My loving grandmother, Betty Lyons McReynolds, translated a grand thought, "Do unto others as though you are the others."

The loving kindness of the community has surrounded us with support and encouragement ad unspeakable joy.

Adding to the happiness of others, we add to our own. Love has no limits. The more we share and give, the more there is to use and absorb.

Being willing to be vulnerable during times of surprise and silence is the spiritual foundation to permanent connection to ourselves and God.

This act of acceptance will deepen and transform us to joyful life. The more Christ-consciousness we direct into our soul, the higher is its frequency.

Being on top or on the bottom, being the most or the least does not matter. Journeys to the bottom come quietly as Carl Sandburg wrote "as little cat's feet."

When our love ends up in disaster, we sing, "I don't know where we both went wrong, but the feelings gone, and I just can't get it back again." Love that goes away might really be another pleasure trip, an ecstatic high, a grand illusion. The combination of circumstances to create anything real comes at another's expense. Everything that was imagined as a wonderful life rescue ends up self-defeating in the long run. Nobody can love you like God can.

Close relationships are blighted and broken, and finally ended because our illusive concepts of joy as a feeling become a command performance. One unfinished soul once told me, "Love is a feeling and sex is a sport."

Joy comes as a person is free, faithful, and quiet, free of coercion and demand. Pursuing the pleasures of the present day, we cannot perceive tomorrow.

Tomorrow arrives persistently and we find ourselves regretful, lonely, and bankrupt.

Joy endures to quench a deeper thirst. Listen to the silence between words. Let silence surround you.

Life is present in the world as silence. Pay attention.

Discern about who you choose to give out your energy. No soul can be still within without giving attention to the gift of silence.

Intuit a moment of surprise as a drop of water falls on your soul's center. Another drop falls. Feelings arrange themselves in order around us, and we finally feel the warmth. Memories and thoughts line up like academy cadets in proper order at West Point. Joy mingles with guilt, anxiety, anger, and fear. Painful memories and our dark nights of our souls transform into compassion for others. Life is not a problem to be solved, but a mystery to be lived with joy.

When a friend gets out of touch for long periods of time, the friend can't wait to talk or contact or visit. Nothing can relieve anxiety that we feel as much as an open conversation with a beloved friend who understands us.

It is so dangerous to risk sharing ourselves with a stranger. Unknown people can manipulate or seduce us. A loving friend creates a relaxing atmosphere in which we can talk in confidence about doing or not doing a task, or going or not going where we think the joy is. Love helps us to preserve the integrity of the relationship.

Deep appreciation causes us to co-experience what our friends are feeling and thinking.

When other people become rude, crude, or indifferent, when they wound us or when we wound them, we need a friend to help us sort things out.

Friends are like two thirsty people crossing a desert looking for a refreshing oasis.

Life stressors threaten the most loving relationships. When we are reeling, we must keep talking, keep lines of communication open. Accept the low times and the joy times. Unconditional love comes without wings. Love never flies away. Love is the cement of life that binds us all together.

The writer and wise guide, Ralph Waldo Emerson said, "Happiness is a perfume you cannot pour on others without getting a few drops on yourself." Catch the joy as it flies.

From a foundation of grace, our souls experience God's working in us. We enjoy knowing the miraculous ways that rebellious, unwanted, and unexpected serendipitously are woven into our souls and the souls of others.

Those who stand with us in our confusion become grace personified.

Jesus said that we are the salt of the earth. He taught us how to live in this world. Read Matthew 5:13-16. He used two words salt and light. Jesus is speaking to unfinished souls who place their faith in him. We are not isolationists. If we withdraw from the world, they have no effect. We are not conformists. We are called to be in the world, but not of it. John 17:16 and Romans 12:1-2.

Jesus' main point follow his assertion that believers are salt. "If salt loses its flavor, how shall it be seasoned?" How does salt lose strength? Having lived much of my life in Nebraska, a state that receives quite a lot of snow each winter, I know salt loses its potency. It happens when snow gets wet. As snow begins to fall, Nebraska cities send road crews into action putting salt on the streets. In the beginning, salt works well. As the snow to fall and melt, salt becomes diluted. When it does, the salt loses the battle. Snow piles high.

If salt becomes defiled or corrupt by having to use sand to increase the supply. When a snowstorm hits unexpectedly, the impure salt does little good. "It is then good for nothing but to be thrown out and trampled underfoot by men."

Jesus says we are like salt and light. Light dispels darkness. We see things as they really are. We are the revelation of God for others.

Shining our light, the world sees our good works. Our light glorifies our Father in heaven. Read Galatians 6:9-10, James 2:14-20. When we do good deeds, our light shines and God receives the glory and praise.

Conversion's blessings root us into the love that makes the implausible plausible, the improbable probable, the impossible possible. Passionate joy keeps our little lives from lessoning the value of God living in our souls. The spiritual life is God-life. Passionate joy involves living our entire lives in God. We will finish what God has begun in us. We cannot nurture, cultivate, or grow it by ourselves. God has designed the process. We possess the resources. Read Philippians 1:6 and 2:13.

God can finish our soul God brings us faultless and flawless into divine Presence. (See my book *Passionate Joy: Building a Wealth of Joy in a World Starved for Love* by Universe Press.)

Building a wealth of joy means to eliminate the mass starvation of love. Jouissance is my favorite French word. It was first used by Jacques Lacan, therapist in Paris. The word means radical and excessive joy. It is a word that means "going to the roots."

The first and great commandment illuminates our passion for God. Read Matthew 22:34-40, Mark 1:28-31, Luke 10:25-28. Jesus' own expectation of spiritual passion and a clear definition of the spiritual life.

The finishing soul loves God with the heart, soul, mind, and strength. Faithful Jews repeated Deuteronomy 6:5 several times a day. It is called the Shema. What we love controls us.

Love is a word that we understand intuitively and immediately. Love for God is a specific kind of love reserved for God. That God-life is contested by self-life.

Bernard of Clairvaux cited four types of love: Love for self's sake. Love of God for self's sake. Love of God for God's sake. Loving God for self's sake. Bernard gives us the keys for loving God fully. Love God with everything you've got, with all you are, have, and know.

God deeply desires our love.

Gifts, words, and deeds for God require time, money, and energy that the unfinished soul would rather shower on other loves. God does not want us to feel the anxiety that we feel in the disjunction between loving God and loving people. Married people realize that when their relationship with their spouse is healthy, everything else is better.

Soul passion is soul satisfaction. Love for Jesus exceeds love for sinning. Offenses offend God. We are estranged from God as we are sinning.

We must have a longing to never sin again. Sin stifles soul love for God. Some sins are easy to do. Some sins do not bother the conscience.

Rejection of sins is natural and premeditated in the grace of God. Read II Peter 1:2-4.

Our mentors, family, and friends bless our souls with hugs, prayers, tears of joy, thumbs up, and grins. Passion for God is not a private matter.

## Biblical words for love

Four words for love are found in the Greek language. Philos stands for brotherly love. This friendship love makes time, corrects errors, forgives faults, and keeps on loving.

Eros is the Greek word for sexual sensual love, reserved in the Holy Scripture for the love between husband and wife.

Agape is the term Jesus used for unconditional, unselfish, and unattached love. Based on a decision to love, it is a passion from the heart. It denotes that a person keeps on loving God.

Loving God with all your soul means an overlapping word for both heart and soul, the fount of free decisions. Agape is the purpose to love God under the direction of the will in personal, self-giving commitment.

And God loves us because.

When my lovely wife celebrated her 80th year birthday, I wrote 80 reasons why I love her.
Laurel has been my inspiration I think about our lives together often. By the time I finished my list, I know I could write down 80 more.

We cherish our commitment while overlooking our struggles.
God loves us, not because of anything that we have done to be loved.
God loves us because God is love.

God is love whether we are joy filled with faith or if we fail to see God moving on our behalf. God is love whether we give all to those in need or if we need constant assurance.

The distinctiveness of Christian love is christocentricism. We are just to learn about Christ in theory. In both meanings of the word. Jesus is the most unique and perfect example of love. We can grow to love as he loves. Read John 13:34.

God is love whether we grow in grace or finish our unfinished souls. Know we can list scores of reasons why we need grace. God desires to embrace us in love, to descend upon us to make us complete and masterpieces of love. With faith we discover his image in the revealed Word. In faith we will start to absorb Jesus' thoughts and desires.

Christian love is the love of Christ in us. Jesus is the way, the truth, and the life. The quality and magnitude of our love are determined by faith. We can love fully only when we perceive ourselves as longing for sanctification, and when you desire to ooze this love into others. We can give Christ to others to the extent that we accept Christ and to the extent we allow Christ to encompass us.

God who is the only love and only good, wants to love us boundlessly. God is always seeking souls, to flood them with the ocean of love. One cannot love the whole community without loving God. When, through faith, we open ourselves to Christ, he becomes our way, truth, and life.

Growing in faith and grace causes a clarification of our finished soul, because Christ then gives us more supernatural light.

Without that supernatural joy, when we gather to meet, the friendship itself may die or slowly become unstitched. It becomes a once upon a time friendship.

Faithful and long friendships share both difficulties and successes. It is the joy-filled soul who still has their first friend.
Friendship lasts a lifetime. A friend knows all about us and loves us anyway. A friend allows us distance but is never far away. Read

Ecclesiastes 6:16. When we give a gift of red roses, they soon wilt and die. Friendship is forever," What a friend we have in Jesus."

On the church sign a Lutheran church worshippers leave seeing the words: "You might just be one person in the world, but you might be the world to just one person."

We have no idea what we are capable of doing. The love of God is opening our eyes to the amazing possibilities that is enfolding in our being. God lights a fire within us that is warm and bright. "This little light of mine" keeps shining long after our days on earth are gone.

God never gives up on us. God gives us the courage to embrace plans that give us a future and a hope. (Matthew Kelly, *Rediscover the Saints*, p. 15)

Souls have differing experiences of the love of God. In each unique event, there are personal meanings and mysteries. Read Matthew 7:7-8. God is keenly interested in every aspect of our lives. God does not stand by the road and wait on our unfinished souls to catch up. God leads us step-by-step where our divine calling is.

My world travels mess with my living routines like prayer, diet, exercise, sleep, and communion with friends and family. Jesus reminds us frequently that we are all children. Without deeply rooted routine we become disoriented and lose sight of what is important. That's how we enjoy amazing friendship with God. Love rearranges priorities.

The unfinished soul may be sleeping, but it is not dead. We can learn to live life on a whole new level. We need to listen to our dissatisfactions, and find what God is saying. This takes boldness and courage.

# Chapter Nine

# Souls Finding Freedom From Sin

In the beginning, God wanted humans to remain free from sin. Our soul integration with God was founded

on our creation in the image and likeness of God. Prior to humans choosing to sin, the first humans lived in original innocence.

They were integrated into harmony with God. The hinge of temptation to sin came with ambition and fear. Read Genesis 3:4-5. Faith was replaced with fear. Humans wanted to be like God. And, in fact, they are. They became deceived by pride.

They denied God's infinitude and their finitude. Their motivation was prideful self-love. Humans freely committed original sin. God in love does not override human freedom. Being bound by sin causes anxiety, haste, and a wounding of th e love of Jesus.
Read Genesis 3:17-19.

We resist granting and receiving forgiveness, a paradox of our unfinished dark souls.

When we take the spiritual fight to freedom into our own sins and we want to try to solve them on our own, we are simply counting on ourselves. There is then no room for faith. Faith relies on God. Without faith, we are pushing Jesus aside. Seekers in faith live in the present moment, sanctifying it as a means of grace. Live as if it is your last day. Tomorrow is not certain. Yesterday does not belong to you. Only today is ours. God does not want us to worry about the future. Looking back to the past or to the future keeps us from living in the present. We lose the grace of the moment.

Anxieties that cause worry about the past or future are trials of faith. Anxiety is always flowing from self-love. Conversion is the fruit of spiritual life. It is "the joy of the Lord" that gives unfinished souls freedom, not at the start, but at the finish.

Our community relationships draw out the best and worst within us. Human love is never flawless.

Insecurity in our relationships can cause us an unhealthy clinging to another, a longing to merge, but fear intimacy.

Unresolved conflict and guilt are causes of depression in later life. It is as common as the cold. We want to finish this life at peace and in our own bed. Facing the past, including our sinfulness, is not to be put off to our deathbeds. The words I spoke to my brother David were asking him to forgive me of any and all things I did that might have hurt him. I ask him to do the same for me. I told him how much I loved him. God never demands that we get it right all the time. We are to acknowledge our sins, our faults, our mistakes, and make amends when we can.

## Sin and Freedom for the Soul

Sinful acts include abuse, hatred, greed, dishonesty, violence, cheating, lying, and failure to do what is the right thing. The soul enslaved by sin cannot be healed if one denies that these acts are our responsibility.

Sin is entrenched in us. Our sinful acts are premeditated. Sin is a habit that we cannot control. Paul admitted that he did not understand his acts. I do what I do not want to do, but the evil I do not desire to do, this I keep on doing, he wrote. Good habits free us. When sin is a habit, souls lose freedom.

Our only hope is not for more willpower. Our hope comes from a new set of habits. It is only by surrendering to God and the ways and thoughts and wills that our souls can experienced freedom. We stumble and fall as we are not finished and sanctified. Jesus is our perfect and finished Savior. He forgives us of sin.

Ultimately only the offer and acceptance of forgiveness will be the healing. Forgiveness gives the ability to live with the past without

71

being enslaved it. Read Matthew 18:22. Pray for the grace to want to forgive. Withholding forgiveness makes us continue to suffer. We are he losers every time.

We are released from the tragic happening that still control us. Forgiveness is as important to the person who forgives as it is for the one who is forgiven.

Forgiveness is not simple. It is quite complex. It takes time to consider all its layers. The emphasis of the New Testament is on forgiveness of sins, reconciliation, and living made possible by the love of God through Christ. Read Matthew 7:21, Colossians 3:13, Romans 14:7-10.

Sin breaches relationships, causing alienation, separation, and estrangement. The possibility of oneness is lost. Forgiveness frees us and we draw closer to God and others to whom we are indebted. The Spirit of Joy and love free us from a painful past to a new future. Only forgiveness sets us free.

"I believe in the forgiveness of sins" were ancient words in the Apostles' Creed. The ultimate aim of the intervention of God in the realm of the unfinished soul is salvation. God is an equal opportunity forgiver. Forgiveness is God's solidarity with sinners. It is an invitation to celebrate at the banquet.

Forgive us as we forgive others.

The heart and soul of the Lord's Model Prayer is forgiveness. We cannot expect to be forgiven by God if we are not willing to forgive others. The Scottish translation of the prayer says, "forgive us our debts as we forgive our debtors. Forgiveness sets individual and community on an equal footing.

English translators used the phrase differently. "Forgive our trespasses as we forgive those who trespass against us." The people in Scotland had no trespassing laws. So, translators took the liberty to use the word "debts." Today many Christians just use the word "sins." Life goes wrong when boundaries are not respected. Broken fences must be mended.

Older souls experience a self-contempt for we feel it difficult to forgive ourselves. If God has forgiven us, why do we find it so hard to forgive ourselves?

Let me share some coaching or counseling suggestions. Are there things from your past where we are nursing grudges? How will we forgive and move on? Is there somebody with whom my soul has unfinished business? Let the Holy Spirit help us sort it out.

The foundation of sin lies in lack of trust in God. This has been true from the beginning of history. The biblical account tells us the first humans were attacked by the evil being in the seeds for distrust.

We are being seduced to believe that God is not love. We feel threatened. We are confused and afraid. If our souls are not freed from sin, they experience anxiety, fear, and guilt as they are tempted by the seeds of mistrust.

The redeeming work of Christ continues as Jesus redeems us from fear. We must be oriented to more openness to salvation. We must open ourselves. Grace never stops. Faith is the acceptance and the process of accepting Christ.

It is witnessing a miracle. Read Luke 17:6. By stirring within your soul acts of faith, you will in each situation entrust yourself as a child into the arms of the loving Father. If you trust in God, you will sever the root of that which is destroying you. Through the consequences of sin will you see how far you have strayed.

Conversion to the attitude of a child is the imperative condition for entering into the kingdom of God. Read Matthew 18:3. That clearly means awaiting, being humble, and trusting like a child.

Childlikeness means not depending on ordinary human effort It is a stirring in the heart for something, a hunger which a child would call a surprise. Childlike faithfulness hungers for a miracle. One can be 80 years old, as I am, and remain young. God is always young. Constant predicting and calculating are traits of old age.

God needs your childlike faith for performing miracles as nothing is impossible for God. Read Mark 9:24.

God is always young and amazing. Experiencing God is living in amazement and joy as a child.

Jesus' parable of the prodigal son is deliberately unfinished. If the prodigal does not return as a child, but as a hired worker, then he will leave again and again. A son who has the soul of a hired worker will not be amazed by love. The son in the parable did not perceive the wounding of his father. He never experienced compassion for his father's deep pain.

A finished soul becomes a child. God's love is a joy-filled surprise. When we become conscious of our sinfulness, we look upon Jesus' wounds as nothing. There was no contrition in the prodigal son.

Conversion is an eternal and basic dimension of faith. Conversion keeps our faithing from becoming static. Conversion is not a single act but is a process. We are free from evil and sin.

Self-love is replaced by childlike God love. Our faith must continue to develop through the permanent process of conversion. No soul is doomed. No sin is final.

God induces us to desire forgiveness. God does not remember the wounds inflicted by us. If you are far from God, you are always invited to return. God is waiting while we are sinning.

God and the angels in heaven rejoice over one sinner who has turned and known the mercy of the Lord. The Bible is continually calling us to do what we cannot do. We cannot forgive, but as we try to forgive, we are given the gift of God's forgiveness. There are not enough days in human existence on earth to heal an unfinished soul. There are not enough years in history for all the sins to be forgiven. God has time for human restoration. In God's eternal time everything is completed.

When we are weak and sinful, you can crawl up into Jesus' arms. Jesus is the Good Shepherd.

He is looking for lost sheep. Faithing makes us grateful for the unconditional love.

Sins can be sins of negligence as well as openly committed. God sees the sins of negligence as the worst.

Freedom from sin is both intoxicating and frightening. To blame others for our poor choices means we are faultless. Nothing is as exhilarating as freedom of choice. We have freedom to make mistakes, to miss the mark.

Soul's sensing freedom from sin by faith and grace experience belovedness of a child of God. This newfound freedom runs counter to the mandate that many of us grew up with. True freedom takes us beyond the aura of coercion to choosing love.

# Chapter Ten

# Souls Keeping The Joy Of God

When I celebrated my "retirement," the church was full of grace and love, celebrating joy and happiness. These souls gave me a taste of joy as they came to celebrate and affirm the goodness of life and love.

As we left the sanctuary together, we sang, "Joyful, joyful we adore thee." I wore the robe with doctoral stripes, my brightest stole with "joy" stitched into the fabric. Our mission was again shared: "to create an atmosphere where joy and miracles happen." We renewed the invitation to weave our lives and our love into the world as affirmation and celebration of the life God has given us all.

Many had experienced the mysterious working of God in their lives. Some had never known Jesus' joy. They had journeyed from great difficulty to new freedom. The sweet loving child on the cover of this book represents scores of souls born into the kingdom with professions of new faith and baptism.

## Stepping Back to See

We often become aware of the mysterious working of God in our lives in retrospect. When a soul has journeyed through difficulties to new freedom, from turmoil and division to the ups and downs of daily life, we are in the vantage point of grace.

During that time, we sense the movement of God like we never have before. I see this by looking at photographs in my scrapbooks of unforgettable events in the churches where God has placed me. In my prayers I shed tears for the moments of grace. We become aware of the deeper love that surrounded us.

Friends, families, and companions become vital in the larger community of faith. The invisible love of God is made visible.
Grace is personified. Scripture tells us that we consist of body, soul, and spirit. Read I Thessalonians 5:23. Our material bodies are evident. Souls and spirits are less distinguishable. The word soul as the Greeks use it implies our mind, will, and deepest desires as seen in personal preferences, choices, and emotional responses to situations in life.

The Greek word for spirit refers to way we connect and communicate with God. Spirit differs from soul. Spirit points toward and exists exclusively for God. The unfinished soul is self- centered. Our spirit experiences comfort, peace, and joy in the presence of God. To be fully alive is to realize the joy of God overflows within. Read John 10:10.

Keeping the joy of God is reciprocal as joy weaves us more closely together. We experience the communion of saints. This togetherness reaches through the ages to draw upon the wisdom of those who have lived fully and faithfully. This communion is inclusive of those living in our current lives. This togethering reaches to those who have yet to come into our lives. Even those we do not know personally.

The world is a barrier and at the same time is the passageway to joy. When joy is awakened in our unfinished souls, the world can become the place from which joy is received to everyone everywhere.

Spiritual fulfillment is the destiny and heritage. Joy is a given. It is on an eternal level. Keeping the joy from God is a choice allowing us to complete spiritual fulfillment. Joy filled souls know who they are, and they choose what they already have been chosen to possess. Have faith that our spiritual fulfillment is there for us, even if we do not see it. Be patient. Be joyful. Be kind. Be in the Spirit's loving embrace.

To dance with joy is to find we differ from reasonable expectations. The outer world is a mirror of our inner thoughts. We change the outer world by changing the inner one. Bodies are physical, composed of matter that is limited by time and space.

Many who have become frustrated with the frequently dysfunctional patters of the institutional church, have bled with us and

thanked us in saying our ministry had been a blessing, a sign of hope and healing. The Spirit of Joy Church, whatever it is called and wherever it is, gives a taste of what the community of faith could be. Those who believe in the mystery and the promise remind us that our lives are not separate but are woven together in our hurts as well as our hopes. Joy is not the absence of suffering, but it is the presence of God.

Love is the foundation. Jesus is love incarnate. God's love reaches beyond distances and differences.

Joy is a small word carrying a big gift.

Joy delights in the divine. Read Psalm 34:8. God's delight is safely tucked into our souls. Joy is not meant to be elusive. God is good all the time. This joy is everlasting, glorious, and inexpressible Read I Peter 1:7-9.

Joy is bigger than our vision of a perfect life. Joy delights in God's perfection and even our own imperfection. God keeps a record of our imperfections with the goal of our soul's encounter with who God really is. Read Psalm 56:7-9.

Joy and faith are forever linked. The gift of joy is irrepressible sunshine. Joy is light is the dark days as the warmth of Love overwhelms us.

Nothing is impossible. When things in life become insurmountable, we know the race is not over yet. Read Hebrews 12:1-2.

Joy is there when we become stuck. Self-pity offers us a seat. Finding the joy, we long for is found in God who loves us. Having joy based on who God is, changes our perspective about earthly circumstances. "The joy of the Lord" releases the weight of what is keeping us from receiving the joy of who Christ is in your soul. We act because we are loved, not the other way around. Joy follows as our soul is set free.

Whatever is happening now, whether woeful or wonderful, is not bigger than the gift of joy and grace. We receive strength and understanding to keep joy through the power of the Holy Spirit. This divine gift awakens something miraculous. The soul will sing, sour, and start to laugh, noted by our tears of faithful surprise.

As I pray and spend time with people who desire to rejoice in God with me, I find encouragement. Read Isaiah 61:10. Taking steps to obey God feels difficult. Souls are filled with joy as we seek godly counsel from a wise friend or mentor, a licensed mental health practitioner, and those who walk along with us in our soul journey to joy.

Elizabeth Kubler Ross said, "It is only when we truly know and understand that we have a limited time on earth, and we have no way of knowing when our time is up that we will begin to live each day to the full, as if it were the only one day we had."

Being forgiven, loved, and free will inspire us to live by faith, courage, compassion, and integrity. God gives us gifts we do not deserve, so we will know God in ways that we cannot deny.

"Joyful, joyful, we adore thee" was written by Henry Van Dyke. It is never too late to finish making our souls with joy. Joy is Jesus' plan for us. The Greek word implies "to be made perfect."

Joy is second in the list of the fruit of the Spirit. Looking closely at the reek word for grace, we find that gift is at the heart of grace. In college years, I took courses in Latin, German, and Greek, which I knew I would need for serious theological study. I found Greek was a highly infected language. When reading Greek for understanding we focus on a root word. When we add prefixes and suffixes, we discover many related words and nuances. Gratitude. Grace. Gift. Forgiveness. Joy.

Joy is a product of grace. God gives the gift of grace. Joy is the laughter of an unfinished soul. We delight in the loving fellowship with Christ. We feel secure in the love of God.

Joy is the soul-making experience in the intersection of the nature of God and the soul's openness.

Ask God to help you listen to the voice that joyfully fills the soul. Follow that path. Unearth the passions in your heart.

Life is short. Our time to gladden the souls who travel with us is brief. Love now.

"Make Me an Instrument of Thy Peace" written by Francis of Assisi is a guide for an unfinished soul.

"Lord, make me an instrument of thy peace. "Where there is hatred, let me sow love.

Where there is injury, pardon. Where there is doubt, faith.

Where there is despair, hope. Where there is darkness, light. Where there is sadness, joy.

"O divine Master, grant that I may not so much seek to be consoled as to console,

To be understood as to understand, To be loved as to love.

"For it is in giving that we receive.
It is in pardoning that we are pardoned.
It is in dying to self that we are born to eternal life."

# Bibliography

Atwell, Robert. *Soul Unfinished*. Brewster, Massachusetts: Paraclete Press, 2012.

Barron, Robert. *To Light a Fire on the Earth: Proclaiming the Gospel in a Secular Age*. New York: Penguin Random House, 2019.

Biga, Leo Adam, "John Cook Knows Darkness He Has Located the Light," Flatwater Free Press, April 23, 2022.

Bonhoeffer, Dietrich. *The Cost of Discipleship*. New York: Harper and Row, 1956.

Bransfield, Brian. *Life Everlasting: The Mystery and the Promise*. Boston: Pauline Books, 2010.

Caulfield, Sean. *The Experience of Praying*. New York: Paulist Press, 1988.

D'Arcy, Paula. *A New Set of Eyes*. New York: Crossword Publishing Company, 2002.

Fosdick, Harry Emerson. *The Meaning of Prayer*. Nashville: Abingdon Press reprint from 1915, 1964.

Gee, Judee. *Intuition: Awakening Your Inner Guide*. New York: Barnes and Noble, 1999.

Gire, Ken. *Windows of the Soul: Experiencing God in New Ways*. Grand Rapids, Michigan: Zondervan Publishing House, 1996.

Jones, Alan. *Soul Making: The Desert Way of Spirituality*. San Francisco: Harper & Row, Publishers, 2007.

Jones, Gregory. *Embodying Forgiveness: A Theological Analysis*. Grand Rapids, Michigan: William B. Eerdmans Publishing Company, 1995.

Kelly, Matthew. *Perfectly Yourself: Discovering God's Dream for You.* North Palm Beach, Florida: Beacon Publishing Company, 2006.
Kelly, Matthew. *Rediscover the Saints.* North Palm Beach, Florida: Blue Sparrow Books, 2020.

Kelsey, Morton. *Transcend.* New York: Crossword Press, 1981.

Kierkegaard, Soren. *Purity of Heart Is to Will One Thing.* New York: Harper and Row, 1956.

Killinger, John. *Bread for the Wilderness, Wine for the Journey.* Waco, Texas: Word Press, 1976.

Lama, Dalai and Desmond Tutu. *The Book of Joy.* New York: Penguin Random House, 2016.

Markova, Dawna. *I Will Not Die an Unlived Life.* Boston: Conari Press, 2010.

McReynolds, James. *Soul Mating: A Premarital Marriage and Relationship Manuel.* New York: Better Life Publishers, 1980.

McReynolds, James, *The Joy of Prayer: The Way to Intimacy with God.* Cleveland, Tennessee: Parson's Porch Books, 2020.

McReynolds, James. *The Joy of Preaching: Encountering Jesus through the Word of God.* Cleveland, Tennessee: Parson's Porch Books, 2013.

McReynolds, James. *The Joy of the Kingdom.* Cleveland, Tennessee: Parson's Porch Books, 2020.

McReynolds, James. *Visionquest of Joy: The Least Discussed Human Emotion.* Bryn Mawr, Pennsylvania: Dorrance and Company, Incorporated, 1988.

Miller, Calvin. "Keeping an Ear to the Ground of Being," *The Baptist Student,* May 1977.

Moore, Thomas. *Care of the Soul: A Guide for Cultivating Depth and Sacredness in Everyday Life*. New York: Harper Collins, Publishers, 1992.

Morris, Robert. "Listening for the Voice," *Weavings: A Journal of the Christian Spiritual Life*. Number 3, pp. 10-11, August 2010.

Ornish, Dean. *Love and Survival: Eight Pathways to Intimacy and Health*. New York: Harper/Perennial, 1999.

Ortberg, John. *Soul Keeping: Caring for the Most Important Part of You*. Grand Rapids, Michigan: Zondervan Books, 2014.

Reynolds, William. *Joyful Sound*. New York: Holt, Rinehart, and Winston, 1978.

Saward, John. *Sweet and Blessed Country: The Christian Hope for Heaven*. Oxford: Oxford University Press, 2008.

Street, Alan. *Heaven on Earth: Experiencing he Kingdom of God in the Here and Now*. Eugene, Oregon: Harvest House Publishers, 2013.

Weatherhead, Leslie. *The Significance of Silence*. New York: Abingdon-Cokesbury, 1945.

Willimon, William. *Rekindling the Flame: Strategies for a Vital United Methodism*. Nashville: Abingdon Press, 1987.

Willard, Dallas. *Renovation of the Heart*. Colorado Springs, Colorado: NavPress, 2002.

Wright, N. T. *Justification: God' Plan and Paul's Vision*. Downers Grove, Illinois: Inter/Varsity Press, 2009.

# Notes About The Author

The Rev. Dr. James McReynolds, age 80, has been called the minister of joy to the world.

Millions throughout the world have read his books. Others have listened to his radio and television programs and blog casts. Millions have heard Jim preach throughout the world. Jim's books have been translated into more than 30 languages.

When serving as information specialist for the Sunday School Board of the Southern Baptist Convention, he became a prolific writer. He wrote articles for Baptist Press, major newspapers and magazines, newsletters, and printed sermons.

Jim has earned nine academic degrees including five doctorates. Carson-Newman University, Baylor University, the University of Missouri, Midwestern Baptist Theological Seminary, Vanderbilt University, and the University of Oxford enhanced the development of his soul and his international ministry.

Born in Kingsport, Tennessee, he began his preaching and writing work as a twelve-year-old living in Bristol, Tennessee. Jim expresses his love for coming home. A ministry that expands 70 years and millions of miles. There is joy and wonder when we come home. "When I lived in Bristol, I could not imagine leaving Bristol, whose motto spans State Street between Virginia and Tennessee. The sign reads, 'A good place to live.'

"Making my home and sharing in many places, I now enjoy the 'Good Life,' as Nebraska's state motto reads. I have lived in Nebraska from 1985-1992 and then moved back to Nebraska to dwell from 1998 until today."

Jim has preached more sermons, wrote more books, and counseled more people in the state of Nebraska than any other state or nation. The Spirit has led him to call Nebraska home for 32 years until now.

This book is an attempt for readers who have unfinished souls to eat the fruit of the Spirit.

www.ingramcontent.com/pod-product-compliance
Lightning Source LLC
Chambersburg PA
CBHW051008140626
46546CB00016B/1344